# Grundschulwörterbuch Englisch

Von Kirstin Jebautzke
Mit Bildern von Nina Dulleck

Übersetzen

Spielen

Wiederholen

Spiel verlassen

Ravensburger

# Vorwort

**Liebe Schülerin, lieber Schüler,**

das Wörterbuch, das du hier in den Händen hältst, ist viel mehr als ein Buch zum Nachschlagen von englischen Wörtern – tiptoi macht Englischlernen zum Erlebnis.

## Sich in die Sprache einhören – Mit tiptoi sprechen die Seiten wie Muttersprachler

Sicherlich weißt du schon längst, dass man eine Sprache besonders dann gut lernen kann, wenn man ein sprachliches Vorbild hat – mit dem tiptoi-Stift hältst du das Vorbild direkt in der Hand:
Auf den Themenbildern zu Beginn jedes Kapitels kannst du einzelne Bildausschnitte mit dem tiptoi-Stift antippen, um herauszufinden, wie sie auf Englisch heißen. Du kannst Dinge und Personen auch mehrmals antippen. Wenn du eine Person ein zweites Mal antippst, wird sie dir sogar etwas erzählen. Alle englischen Sounds sind mit englischen Muttersprachlern eingespielt.

## Interaktiv Vokabeln lernen – Mit tiptoi-Vokabelspielen macht es richtig Spaß

In jedem Themenbild steckt außerdem ein interaktives Lernspiel. Hier werden die Vokabeln in immer neuer Mischung gespielt und so zunehmend im Gedächtnis verankert. Tippe dafür auf den orangen Würfel und lass dich überraschen.

**Den eigenen Lernweg gehen – Bei über 5.000 Tippmöglichkeiten hast du die Wahl**

Du willst wichtige Vokabeln zu einem bestimmten Thema gezielt lernen oder nachschlagen? In den thematisch sortierten Kapiteln findest du zu jedem Wort ein kleines Bild, die deutsche Übersetzung und einen Beispielsatz. Alles kannst du einzeln hörbar machen, wenn du mit dem tiptoi-Stift auf das Wort, das Bild oder den Satz tippst. Bei so vielen Möglichkeiten hast du die Wahl: Du kannst einsprachig lernen, du kannst über Bilder lernen oder du kannst dich mit tiptoi selber abfragen. Finde heraus, was für dich die beste Methode ist.

**Gut sortiert – thematisch und alphabetisch**

Die Zusammenstellung der Vokabeln nach Themen passt genau zum Lehrplan deiner Schule. Ganz am Ende des Buches findest du jedoch alle Wörter des Buches auch noch einmal zum einzeln Nachschlagen alphabetisch sortiert: Englisch–Deutsch und Deutsch–Englisch.

Manchmal taucht als Bild das kleine Monster auf. Es wurde immer dann verwendet, wenn eine Zeichnung nicht eindeutig genug sein kann.

# Inhalt


## At home — Seite 6

Themenseite mit Vokabelspiel 6–7
Wortschatz: Familie, Haus, Garten, Möbel, Geschirr 8–21

## At school — Seite 22

Themenseite mit Vokabelspiel 22–23
Wortschatz: Schule, Klassenzimmer, Schulsachen, Fächer 24–31

## At the clothes shop — Seite 32

Themenseite mit Vokabelspiel 32–33
Wortschatz: Im Laden, Kleider, Schuhe, Schmuck 34–41

## At the supermarket — Seite 42

Themenseite mit Vokabelspiel 42–43
Wortschatz: Im Supermarkt, Speisen, Getränke, Obst, Gemüse 44–53

## At the doctor's — Seite 54

Themenseite mit Vokabelspiel 54–55
Wortschatz: Beim Arzt/Tierarzt, Körperteile, Haustiere 56–65

## Sports and hobbies — Seite 66

Themenseite mit Vokabelspiel 66–67
Wortschatz: Hobbies, Sportarten, Auf dem Spielfeld 68–73

## At the zoo — Seite 74

| | |
|---|---|
| Themenseite mit Vokabelspiel | 74–75 |
| Wortschatz: Im Zoo, Wilde Tiere, Auf dem Spielplatz | 76–83 |

## Down at the farm — Seite 84

| | |
|---|---|
| Themenseite mit Vokabelspiel | 84–85 |
| Wortschatz: Auf dem Bauernhof, Bauernhoftiere, Natur | 86–91 |

## In town — Seite 92

| | |
|---|---|
| Themenseite mit Vokabelspiel | 92–93 |
| Wortschatz: In der Stadt, Gebäude, Fahrzeuge, Berufe | 94–103 |

## All year round — Seite 104

| | |
|---|---|
| Themenseite mit Vokabelspiel | 104–105 |
| Wortschatz: Jahreszeiten, Wochentage, Uhrzeit, Feste, Wetter | 106–115 |

| | |
|---|---|
| Zahlen, Farben, Formen | Seite 116 |
| Personalpronomen | Seite 122 |
| Wichtige Verbformen | Seite 122 |
| Fragewörter | Seite 125 |
| Glossar Englisch–Deutsch | Seite 126 |
| Glossar Deutsch–Englisch | Seite 136 |

## At home

## Me and my family

| | | |
|---|---|---|
|  | **is**<br>ist | This is me. |
|  | **family**<br>die Familie | This is my family. |
|  | **mother**<br>die Mutter | I call my mother "Mummy". |
|  | **father**<br>der Vater | I call my father "Daddy". |
|  | **sister**<br>die Schwester | This is my sister Tessa. |
|  | **brother**<br>der Bruder | My brother's name is Nick. |
|  | **baby**<br>das Baby | My little brother Tom is a baby. |
|  | **parents**<br>die Eltern | My mother and my father are my parents. |
|  | **grandmother**<br>die Großmutter | I call my grandmother "Grandma". |
|  | **grandfather**<br>der Großvater | I call my grandfather "Grandpa". |

| | | |
|---|---|---|
|  | **aunt**<br>die Tante | My aunt Helen is tall. |
|  | **uncle**<br>der Onkel | My uncle Paul is big. |
|  | **cousin**<br>der Kusin | I've got two cousins. My cousin Jack and my cousin Susan. |
|  | **wife**<br>die Ehefrau | Mummy is Daddy's wife. |
|  | **husband**<br>der Ehemann | Daddy is Mummy's husband. |
|  | **daughter**<br>die Tochter | My parents have two daughters – Tessa and me. |
|  | **son**<br>der Sohn | My parents have two sons – Nick and Tom. |
|  | **am**<br>bin | I am Emma. I am a girl. |
|  | **are**<br>sind | We are the Miller family. |

## Around the house

**attic**
der Dachboden

We keep many boxes in the attic.

**bathroom**
das Badezimmer

I wash myself in the bathroom.

**bedroom**
das Schlafzimmer

I play and sleep in my bedroom.

**cellar**
der Keller

I don't like to go into the cellar.

**dining room**
das Esszimmer

We eat in the dining room.

**hall**
die Diele

Please take off your shoes in the hall.

**kitchen**
die Küche

We cook in the kitchen.

**living room**
das Wohnzimmer

I watch TV in the living room.

**room**
das Zimmer

There are 6 rooms in our house.

**chimney**
der Schornstein

The chimney is on the roof.

**door**

die Tür

The door is closed.

**doorbell**

die Türklingel

I like the sound of our doorbell.

**fireplace**

der Kamin

We have got a fireplace in the living room.

**front door**

die Haustür

The front door is red.

**garage**

die Garage

The car is in the garage.

**garden**

der Garten

There's a small garden between the houses.

**letterbox**

der Briefkasten

There's a newspaper in the letterbox.

**roof**

das Dach

Two birds are sitting on the roof.

**window**

das Fenster

The window is open.

## In the house

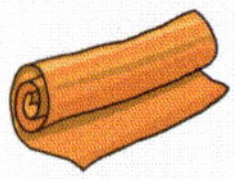

**carpet**
der Teppich

The carpet in Nick‘s room is orange.

**computer**
der Computer

I chat a lot with my friends on the computer.

**desk**
der Schreibtisch

I do my homework at the desk in my bedroom.

**furniture**
die Möbel

We have got some old furniture.

**key**
der Schlüssel

Where is my key?

**radio**
das Radio

Please turn down the radio, it‘s too loud.

**rug**
der Teppich

The rug in front of the sofa is very old.

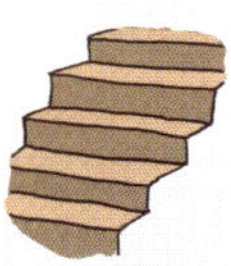

**staircase**
die Treppe

Be careful on the staircase.

**telephone**
das Telefon

The telephone is ringing.

**toys**
die Spielsachen

I have many different toys.

## In the bedroom

**alarm clock**

der Wecker

Every day the alarm clock wakes me up at 7.

**bed**

das Bett

You sleep in a bed.

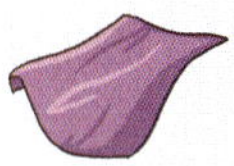

**blanket**

die Decke

You cover yourself with a blanket.

**chest of drawers**

die Kommode

This is a chest of drawers with 3 drawers.

**curtain**

der Vorhang

The curtains in the living room are blue.

**lamp**

die Lampe

Please turn on the lamp, it's getting dark.

**piggy bank**

das Sparschwein

I save my money in a piggy bank.

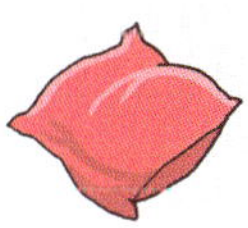

**pillow**

das Kissen

The pillow is very soft.

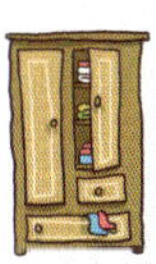

**wardrobe**

der Kleiderschrank

There are a lot of clothes in my wardrobe.

## In the living room

**armchair**

der Sessel

There are two armchairs in the living room.

**bookcase**

das Bücherregal

There is a bookcase in the living room.

**sofa**

das Sofa

The sofa is blue.

**TV**

der Fernseher

We have got a new flat screen TV.

## In the bathroom

**basin**

das Waschbecken

You wash your hands at the basin.

**bathtub**

die Badewanne

I like to take a bath in the bathtub.

**comb**

der Kamm

You comb your hair with a comb.

**hairbrush**

die Bürste

You brush your hair with a hairbrush.

**mirror**

der Spiegel

There's a mirror that you can look in.

| | | |
|---|---|---|
|  | **shampoo**<br>das Shampoo | You use shampoo to wash your hair. |
| 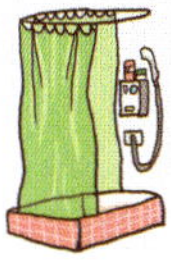 | **shower**<br>die Dusche | Every morning I take a shower. |
|  | **soap**<br>die Seife | Please use soap when you wash your hands. |
|  | **tap**<br>der Wasserhahn | Please close the tap properly. |
|  | **toilet**<br>die Toilette | May I use the toilet, please? |
|  | **toilet paper**<br>das Toilettenpapier | Here‘s a new roll of toilet paper. |
|  | **toothbrush**<br>die Zahnbürste | You clean your teeth with a toothbrush. |
| 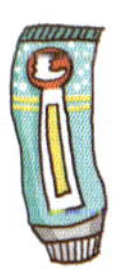 | **toothpaste**<br>die Zahnpasta | Where is the toothpaste? |
|  | **washing machine**<br>die Waschmaschine | The washing machine is in the bathroom. |

## In the kitchen

| | | |
|---|---|---|
|  | **broom**<br>der Besen | Daddy is cleaning the kitchen with a broom. |
| 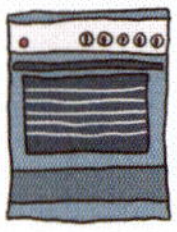 | **cooker**<br>der Herd | Watch out, the cooker can be hot. |
|  | **cup**<br>die Tasse | You drink coffee or tea out of a cup. |
|  | **cupboard**<br>der Küchenschrank | You put cups, pots and plates in a cupboard. |
|  | **dishwasher**<br>die Geschirrspülmaschine | We put the dirty dishes in the dishwasher. |
| 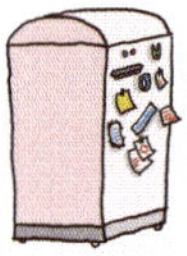 | **fridge**<br>der Kühlschrank | You keep milk and cheese in the fridge. |
| 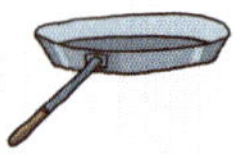 | **pan**<br>die Pfanne | Let‘s make some pancakes in the pan. |
|  | **pot**<br>der Topf | The big pot is for soup.<br>The small pot is for milk. |
|  | **sink**<br>die Spüle | The sink is full of dirty dishes. |
|  | **vacuum cleaner**<br>der Staubsauger | The vacuum cleaner is very loud. |

## Around the table

| | | |
|---|---|---|
|  | **chair**<br>der Stuhl | There are 5 chairs around the table. |
|  | **fork**<br>die Gabel | You eat cake with a fork. |
|  | **glass**<br>das Glas | Can I have a glass of water, please? |
| 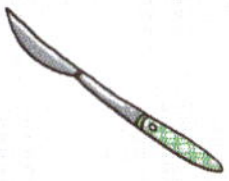 | **knife**<br>das Messer | You cut bread with a knife. |
| 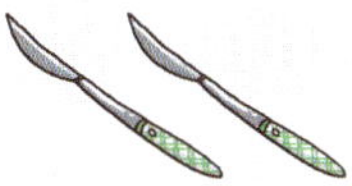 | **knives**<br>die Messer | There are two knives on the plate. |
| 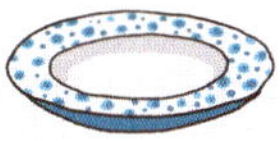 | **plate**<br>der Teller | You eat from a plate. |
|  | **spoon**<br>der Löffel | You eat soup with a spoon. |
|  | **table**<br>der Tisch | This is a round table. |
|  | **teaspoon**<br>der Teelöffel | The small spoon is called a teaspoon. |

## Where is it?

**Where?**
Wo?
Where is the ball?

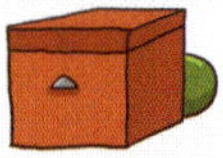

**behind**
hinter
The ball is behind the red box.

**between**
zwischen
The ball is between the 2 boxes.

**in**
in
The ball is in the blue box.

**in front of**
vor
The ball is in front of the blue box.

**near**
in der Nähe von
The ball is near the red box.

**next to**
neben
The ball is next to the blue box.

**on**
auf
The ball is on the red box.

**under**
unter
The ball is under the blue box.

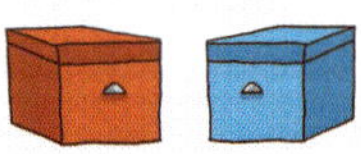

**opposite**
gegenüber
The red box is opposite the blue box.

## What you do at home

**(to) do**
machen
What are you doing?

**(to) do the dishes**
abwaschen
Daddy is doing the dishes.

**(to) dry the dishes**
abtrocknen
I am drying the dishes.

**(to) lay the table**
den Tisch decken
My sister is laying the table.

**(to) look for something**
etwas suchen
Mummy is looking for the key.
Where is it?

**(to) play**
spielen
The baby is playing with a ball.

**(to) sleep**
schlafen
The baby is sleeping.

**(to) tidy up**
aufräumen
My sister is tidying up her room.

**(to) watch TV**
fernsehen
Grandfather is watching TV.

## Where I live

| | | |
|---|---|---|
|  | **address**<br>die Adresse | What's your address? – 5, Portland Street. |
|  | **at home**<br>zu Hause | I am not at home. |
| 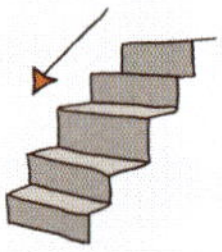 | **downstairs**<br>unten | My bedroom is downstairs. |
|  | **flat**<br>die Wohnung | Do you live in a house or in a flat? |
|  | **house**<br>das Haus | This is our house. I live here. |
|  | **house number**<br>die Hausnummer | What is your house number? |
|  | **(to) live**<br>leben | Where do you live? – In London. |
|  | **neighbour**<br>der Nachbar | Our neighbours are very friendly. |
|  | **street**<br>die Straße | I can play in the street, there are no cars. |
| 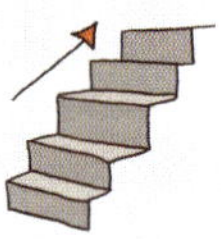 | **upstairs**<br>oben | The bathroom is upstairs. |

## In the garden

**bird house**
das Vogelhaus

I like to watch the birds at our bird house.

**fence**
der Zaun

There's a fence around our garden.

**flower**
die Blume

Have you got flowers in your garden?

**flowerbed**
das Blumenbeet

The flowerbed is very pretty.

**ladder**
die Leiter

You can use a ladder to climb a tree.

**lawn**
der Rasen

I have to cut the lawn every week.

**shed**
das Gartenhaus

The shed is small.

**tree**
der Baum

We have got an old tree in our garden.

**tree house**
das Baumhaus

We built a tree house in the tree.

# At school

Good morning!

## At school

| | | |
|---|---|---|
|  | **lesson**<br>die Schulstunde | We have got many different lessons every day. |
|  | **pupil**<br>der Schüler | Pupils in England wear uniforms. |
|  | **boy**<br>der Junge | Nick is a boy. |
|  | **girl**<br>das Mädchen | Tessa is a girl. |
|  | **teacher**<br>die Lehrerin | The teacher is asking a question. |
|  | **headmistress**<br>die Schulleiterin | The headmistress is in her office. |
|  | **caretaker**<br>der Hausmeister | The caretaker is closing the door. |
|  | **classroom**<br>das Klassenzimmer | The classroom is very big. |
|  | **playground**<br>der Schulhof | During breaktime we play in the playground. |
|  | **gym**<br>die Sporthalle | The new gym is next to our school. |

## Subjects

| | | |
|---|---|---|
|  | **Art**<br>Kunst | My favourite subject is Art. |
|  | **breaktime**<br>die Pause | I like breaktime best. |
|  | **English**<br>Englisch | We learn many new words in English. |
|  | **German**<br>Deutsch | In German we speak a lot. |
| 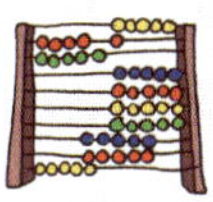 | **Maths**<br>Mathe | We do sums in Maths. |
|  | **Music**<br>Musik | We sing songs in Music. |
|  | **PE** (Physical Education)<br>Sport | We sometimes play football in PE. |
|  | **Social Studies and Sciences**<br>Sachunterricht | We do experiments in Social Studies and Sciences. |
| 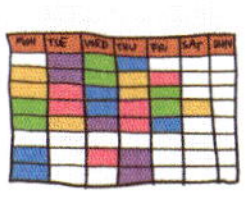 | **timetable**<br>der Stundenplan | My timetable is okay this year. |

## School things

| | | | |
|---|---|---|---|
| 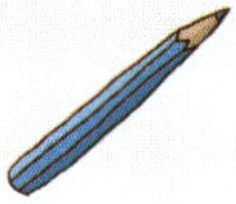 | **coloured pencil** | der Buntstift | I have got six coloured pencils. |
|  | **felt-tip** | der Filzstift | This felt-tip is green. |
|  | **glue** | der Kleber | The glue is very sticky. |
|  | **pen** | der Füller | I have got a red pen. |
|  | **pencil** | der Bleistift | My pencil is very short. |
|  | **pencil case** | die Federmappe | The pencil case is on the desk. |
|  | **rubber** | der Radiergummi | The rubber is red and white. |
|  | **ruler** | das Lineal | Have you got a ruler for me? |
|  | **(a pair of) scissors** | die Schere | You can cut paper with a pair of scissors. |
| 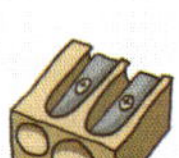 | **sharpener** | der Anspitzer | You sharpen your pencil with a sharpener. |

| | | |
|---|---|---|
|  | **bin**<br>der Papierkorb | Throw the paper in the bin, please. |
|  | **blackboard**<br>die Tafel | Look at the blackboard, please. |
|  | **book**<br>das Buch | Open your book at page 20. |
|  | **calculator**<br>der Taschenrechner | We can use a calculator in Maths. |
|  | **CD player**<br>der CD-Spieler | Put the CD into the CD player, please. |
|  | **chair**<br>der Stuhl | The pupils are sitting on their chairs. |
|  | **chalk**<br>die Kreide | You write with chalk on the blackboard. |
|  | **clock**<br>die Uhr | There's a big clock hanging in the classroom. |
|  | **computer**<br>der Computer | Paul is using the keyboard on the computer. |

## School things

| | | |
|---|---|---|
|  | **computer game**<br>das Computerspiel | Sometimes we play computer games at school. |
|  | **desk**<br>der Schreibtisch | The teacher is sitting at her desk. |
|  | **dictionary**<br>das Wörterbuch | Look up this word in the dictionary, please. |
|  | **dice**<br>die Würfel | It‘s your turn. Throw the dice, please. |
| 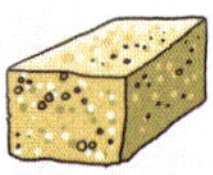 | **eraser**<br>der Tafelschwamm | Clean the blackboard with the eraser, please. |
|  | **exercise book**<br>das Heft | I‘ve forgotten my exercise book at home. |
| 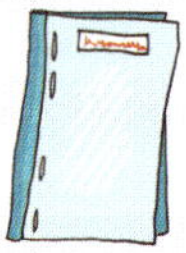 | **folder**<br>der Ordner | The folder for Maths is blue. |
|  | **globe**<br>der Globus | Can you find Germany on the globe? |
|  | **map**<br>die Landkarte | We have got a map of the world at school. |
|  | **paintbrush**<br>der Pinsel | You use a paintbrush for painting pictures. |

| | | |
|---|---|---|
|  | **paintbox**<br>der Malkasten | Don't use too much water in your paintbox. |
|  | **(piece of) paper**<br>das Papier | Please hand out the paper. |
|  | **piano**<br>das Klavier | The teacher is playing the piano at school. |
|  | **pointer**<br>der Zeigestab | Use the pointer to show England on the map. |
|  | **poster**<br>das Poster | There are many posters in the classroom. |
|  | **schoolbag**<br>die Schultasche | Put your book in your schoolbag, please. |
|  | **shelf**<br>das Regal | We keep the scissors on the shelf. |
| 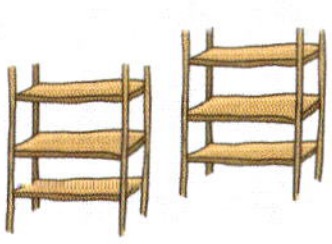 | **shelves**<br>die Regale | There are many books on the shelves. |
| 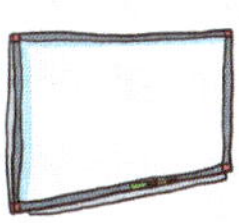 | **board**<br>die Tafel | We've got a board in our classroom. |

## What you do at school

**(to) answer** — Who can answer this question?

antworten

**(to) ask** — Please ask – this question is not easy.

fragen

**(to) colour** — Please colour the little balls in red.

anmalen

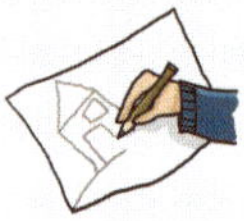

**(to) draw** — Simon doesn't like to draw pictures.

zeichnen

**(to) do Maths** — Sandra is very good at doing Maths.

rechnen

**(to) explain** — Who can explain the question?

erklären

**(to) guess** — Try to guess the answer.

raten

**(to) help** — Can you help David, please?

helfen

**(to) learn** — I want to learn English.

lernen

**(to) listen to** — Now listen carefully to me.

zuhören

| | | |
|---|---|---|
|  | **(to) read**<br>lesen | Please read this text. |
|  | **(to) sing**<br>singen | Let‘s sing a song. |
|  | **(to) sit down**<br>sich hinsetzen | Sit down, please. |
|  | **(to) stand up**<br>aufstehen | Stand up, please. |
|  | **(to) spell**<br>buchstabieren | Can you spell the word: MONSTER? |
|  | **(to) talk**<br>sprechen | Let‘s talk about a new topic. |
|  | **(to) think**<br>denken | Am I pretty or ugly? What do you think? |
|  | **(to) whisper**<br>flüstern | Don‘t whisper with your partner. |
|  | **(to) write**<br>schreiben | Please write a story about this. |

# At the clothes shop

ON
SALE
EMMA

## At the clothes shop

**changing room**
die Umkleidekabine
You can try on the dress in the changing room.

**cheap**
billig
A T-shirt is cheaper than an anorak.

**clothes hanger**
der Kleiderbügel
Put the shirt on the clothes hanger.

**customer**
der Kunde
There are three customers in the shop.

**expensive**
teuer
The dress is very expensive.

**money**
das Geld
Have you got enough money with you?

**price**
der Preis
How much is the price of a new cap?

**price tag**
das Preisschild
The price tag is very small.

**on sale**
im Angebot
The socks are on sale. Let's take some more.

**shop assistant**
die Verkäuferin
The shop assistant is very friendly.

## Clothes and accessories

**anorak**
der Anorak
An anorak is a coat with a hood.

**bathing suit**
der Badeanzug
When you go swimming you need a bathing suit.

**belt**
der Gürtel
A belt can be longer or shorter.

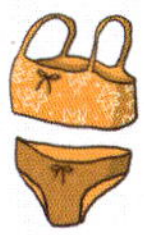

**bikini**
der Bikini
Girls wear bikinis on the beach.

**blouse**
die Bluse
Grandma is wearing a white blouse.

**button**
der Knopf
There are four buttons on the coat.

**cap**
die Kappe
Henry is always wearing his blue cap.

**coat**
der Mantel
Put on your coat – it‘s cold outside.

**dress**
das Kleid
My favourite dress is red.

## Clothes and accessories

| | | |
|---|---|---|
|  | **gloves**<br>die Handschuhe | In winter you put on gloves. |
|  | **hat**<br>der Hut | Some men like to wear hats. |
| 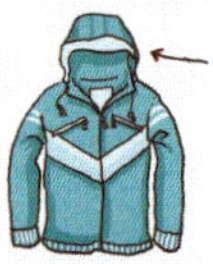 | **hood**<br>die Kapuze | My anorak has got a hood. |
|  | **(a pair of) jeans**<br>die Jeans | I like to wear jeans. |
|  | **mittens**<br>die Fäustlinge | Mittens are warmer than gloves. |
|  | **pullover**<br>der Pullover | At home I always wear my hooded pullover. |
|  | **pyjamas**<br>der Schlafanzug | When you go to bed, you wear pyjamas. |
|  | **raincoat**<br>der Regenmantel | A raincoat keeps you dry when it is raining. |
|  | **scarf**<br>der Schal | To keep your neck warm, you can put on a scarf. |
|  | **shirt**<br>das Hemd | Many men wear shirts. |

| | | |
|---|---|---|
|  | **skirt**<br>der Rock | Some women wear skirts instead of trousers. |
|  | **(a pair of) socks**<br>die Strümpfe | During the summer, I don't wear socks. |
|  | **sweatshirt**<br>das Sweatshirt | This sweatshirt is too big for you. |
|  | **tie**<br>die Krawatte | My Dad never wears a tie. |
|  | **(a pair of) tights**<br>die Strumpfhose | You can wear tights under a dress or a skirt. |
|  | **(a pair of) trousers**<br>die Hose | Most people wear jeans, but there are other trousers. |
|  | **underwear**<br>die Unterwäsche | What colour is your underwear? |
|  | **woolly hat**<br>die Mütze | A woolly hat keeps your head warm in winter. |
|  | **zipper**<br>der Reißverschluss | In most trousers there's a zipper. |

## Footwear

| | | |
|---|---|---|
|  | **(a pair of) boots**<br>die Stiefel | In winter you wear boots. |
|  | **(a pair of) sandals**<br>die Sandalen | In summer you wear sandals. |
|  | **(a pair of) shoes**<br>die Schuhe | What colour are your shoes? |
|  | **(a pair of) slippers**<br>die Hausschuhe | At home you wear slippers. |
|  | **(a pair of) trainers**<br>die Turnschuhe | When you do sports you wear trainers. |
|  | **laces**<br>die Schuhbänder | Many shoes you tie with laces. |

## Wherein you carry things

| | | |
|---|---|---|
|  | **bag**<br>die Tasche | Do you want a paper bag or a plastic bag? |
|  | **handbag**<br>die Handtasche | Mrs Miller wants to buy a new handbag. |
|  | **rucksack**<br>der Rucksack | For hiking you take a rucksack with you. |

**purse** — das Portemonnaie — For my birthday I got a new purse.

**suitcase** — der Koffer — We pack the suitcase for our holidays.

**pocket** — die Hosentasche — What have you got in your pocket?

## Jewellery

**bracelet** — das Armband — You put a bracelet around your arm.

**earring** — der Ohrring — Do you like to wear earrings?

**necklace** — die Kette — You put a necklace around your neck.

**ring** — der Ring — You put a ring on your finger.

**watch** — die Armbanduhr — My watch stopped. What time is it?

## What clothes look like

| | | |
|---|---|---|
|  | **new**<br>neu | I need a new pair of shoes. |
|  | **old**<br>alt | My old shoes have got holes in the soles. |
| 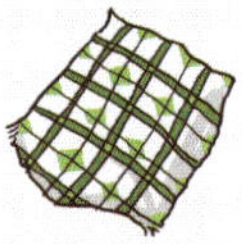 | **plaid**<br>kariert | In Scotland many skirts are plaid. |
|  | **plain-coloured**<br>einfarbig | My mum likes plain-coloured clothes best. |
|  | **pretty**<br>hübsch | This is a very pretty dress. |
|  | **ugly**<br>hässlich | I don't like the blouse. It's ugly. |
|  | **too big**<br>zu groß | The T-shirt is too big for me. |
|  | **too small**<br>zu klein | This T-shirt is too small for me. |
|  | **polka-dotted**<br>gepunktet | I love my polka-dotted dress. |
|  | **striped**<br>gestreift | I don't like my striped dress at all. |

## What you do with clothes

| | | |
|---|---|---|
|  | **(to) put on**<br>anziehen | Put on your raincoat – it‘s raining. |
|  | **(to) take off**<br>ausziehen | Take off your shoes when you enter the house. |
|  | **(to) wear**<br>tragen | Simon is wearing his new shoes. |
|  | **(to) try on**<br>anprobieren | Can I try on these jeans? |
|  | **(to) zip**<br>den Reißverschluss zumachen | The zipper is broken. I can‘t zip it up. |
|  | **(to) tie the laces**<br>Schuhbänder binden | Tie your laces, you might trip over them. |
|  | **(to) buy**<br>kaufen | I want to buy a new pair of trainers. |
|  | **(to) pay**<br>bezahlen | My uncle is paying for my trainers. Thanks! |
|  | **(to) look**<br>aussehen | You look beautiful. |

# At the supermarket

Vegetables
Fruit
Potatoes

## Can you help me?

**How many ...?** How many apples would you like?

Wie viele ...?

**How much ...?** How much is the milk?

Wie viel ...?

**Where is ...?** Where is the sugar?

Wo ist ...?

**Where are ...?** Where are the tomatoes?

Wo sind ...?

**Have you got ...?** Have you got any strawberries?

Haben Sie ...?

**Yes, here you are.** Yes, here you are.

Ja, hier bitte.

**No, sorry.** No, sorry. But we've got grapes.

Nein, leider nicht.

**Do you like ...?** Do you like cheese?

Magst du ...?

**Yes, I do.** Yes, I do. I like cheese.

Ja, mag ich.

**No, I don't.** No, I don't. I don't like cheese.

Nein, mag ich nicht.

## At the supermarket

**aisle**

der Gang

There are many shelves in one aisle.

**bottle**

die Flasche

Do you buy milk in a bottle or a carton?

**entrance**

der Eingang

You come into a shop at the entrance.

**exit**

der Ausgang

You leave the shop at the exit.

**packet**

die Packung

I will take 5 packets of spaghetti. They're on sale.

**shopping basket**

der Einkaufskorb

The shopping basket is empty.

**supermarket**

der Supermarkt

Every Friday I go to the supermarket.

**trolley**

der Einkaufswagen

The trolleys are in front of the supermarket.

**plastic bag**

die Plastiktüte

Put all the groceries in the plastic bag.

## At the supermarket

**open**
geöffnet

The shop is open from 10.00 – 18.00.

**closed**
geschlossen

The supermarket is closed on Sundays.

**crowded**
voll

A lot of people are in the shop. It's crowded.

**empty**
leer

Nobody is there. The shop is empty.

## What you do in a supermarket

**(to) buy**
kaufen

Let's buy some chocolate.

**(to) carry**
tragen

Can you carry the bags? They are heavy.

**(to) go shopping**
einkaufen gehen

Dad doesn't like to go shopping.

**(to) wait in line**
in der Schlange warten

Before we can pay, we have to wait in line.

**(to) push**
schieben

My little son loves to push the trolley.

## Fruit

| | | |
|---|---|---|
|  | **fruit**<br>das Obst | To eat fruit is very healthy. |
|  | **apple**<br>der Apfel | Do you like apples? |
|  | **banana**<br>die Banane | The banana is yellow. |
|  | **cherry**<br>die Kirsche | Cherries are sometimes sour. |
|  | **grapes**<br>die Weintrauben | You can buy green or purple grapes. |
|  | **lemon**<br>die Zitrone | You use lemon in salads. |
|  | **melon**<br>die Melone | Melons contain a lot of water. |
|  | **orange**<br>die Apfelsine | We eat a lot of oranges during the winter. |
|  | **peach**<br>der Pfirsich | Peaches have a very soft skin. |

## Fruit

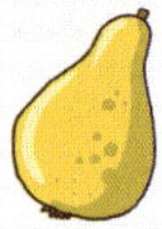

**pear**
die Birne

The pear is very juicy.

**pineapple**
die Ananas

The pineapple is a tropical fruit.

**plum**
die Pflaume

There are many plums on the tree.

**raspberry**
die Himbeere

We grow raspberries in our garden.

**strawberry**
die Erdbeere

My favourite fruit are strawberries.

**watermelon**
die Wassermelone

Watermelons are refreshing during the summer.

## Vegetables

**beans**
die Bohnen

Green beans are very tasty.

**broccoli**
der Brokkoli

Have you ever tried broccoli with cheese?

**cauliflower**
der Blumenkohl

Cauliflower is a white vegetable.

| | | |
|---|---|---|
|  | **carrot**<br>die Karotte | Many children have carrots in their snack box. |
|  | **cucumber**<br>die Gurke | Do you like cucumber salad? |
|  | **lettuce**<br>der Salat | We need a lettuce for the Ceasar salad. |
|  | **mushroom**<br>der Pilz | You can eat raw or fried mushrooms. |
|  | **onion**<br>die Zwiebel | Do you have to cry when you cut an onion? |
|  | **pea**<br>die Erbse | There are many peas in one pea pod. |
|  | **pepper**<br>die Paprika | Peppers can be green, red, yellow or orange. |
| 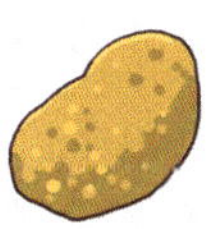 | **potato**<br>die Kartoffel | We eat a lot of potato soup during the winter. |
|  | **tomato**<br>die Tomate | You shouldn‘t keep tomatoes in the fridge. |

## Food

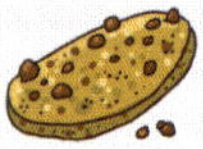

**biscuit** — der Keks — Would you like a biscuit with your tea?

**bread** — das Brot — Yummy, the bread tastes good, when it's fresh.

**butter** — die Butter — Please pass me the butter.

**cheese** — der Käse — This cheese is smelly. I don't like it.

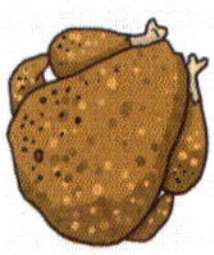

**chicken** — das Hühnchen — Let's have a grilled chicken tonight.

**cornflakes** — die Cornflakes — I eat cornflakes for breakfast.

**chips** — die Pommes frites — Many children like to eat chips.

**chocolate** — die Schokolade — I really like to eat chocolate.

**cream** — die Sahne — If you whip cream too hard, you get butter.

**crisps** — die Chips — Don't eat too many crisps in front of the TV.

**egg**

das Ei

Every Sunday I have an egg for breakfast.

**fish**

der Fisch

Do you like fish?

**flour**

das Mehl

To bake a cake you need flour.

**frozen foods**

die Tiefkühlkost

You must keep frozen foods in the freezer.

**ham**

der Schinken

Can I have a ham sandwich?

**honey**

der Honig

I like honey on my bread.

**ice cream**

das Eis

I love ice cream, especially in the summer.

**jam**

die Marmelade

Grandma makes the best strawberry jam.

**nut**

die Nuss

Some children are allergic to nuts.

## Food

| | | |
|---|---|---|
|  | **marmalade**<br>die Orangenmarmelade | Marmalade is made of oranges. |
| 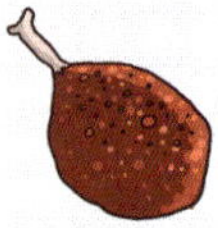 | **meat**<br>das Fleisch | Some people don't eat meat. |
|  | **milk**<br>die Milch | We need two litres of milk. |
|  | **peanut butter**<br>die Erdnussbutter | Do you eat peanut butter for breakfast? |
|  | **pizza**<br>die Pizza | My favourite food is pizza. |
|  | **rice**<br>der Reis | Please buy two packets of rice. |
|  | **roll**<br>das Brötchen | I eat two rolls for breakfast. |
|  | **salami**<br>die Salami | Many children like salami. |
|  | **sandwich**<br>das Sandwich | Can I please have a cheese sandwich? |
|  | **soup**<br>die Suppe | You can buy soup in a tin or in a packet. |

**spaghetti**
die Spaghetti

The spaghetti is hot.

**sugar**
der Zucker

Do you have sugar in your tea?

## Drinks

**coffee**
der Kaffee

Would you like a cup of coffee?

**coke**
die Cola

I don‘t drink coke.

**hot chocolate**
der Kakao

Every morning I drink a hot chocolate.

**juice**
der Saft

Do you like orange juice or apple juice better?

**tea**
der Tee

I don‘t drink black tea.

**water**
das Wasser

Can I have a glass of water, please?

# At the doctor's

ABC
DEFG
HIJK

## At the doctor's

**dentist**

der Zahnarzt

Every year the dentist checks your teeth.

**doctor**

die Ärztin

The doctor is very nice.

**nurse**

die Krankenschwester

The nurse helps the doctor.

**secretary**

die Sekretärin

The secretary checks your name and address.

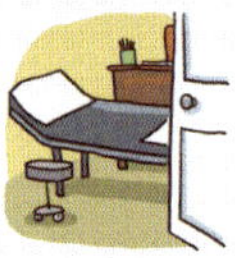

**surgery**

die Arztpraxis

A doctor works in a surgery.

**patient**

der Patient

The patient is waiting for the doctor.

**prescription**

das Rezept

To get medicine you need a prescription.

**pharmacist**

die Apothekerin

A pharmacist makes and sells medicine.

**vet**

der Tierarzt

A vet takes care of ill animals.

**waiting room**

das Wartezimmer

There are many people in the waiting room.

## What happens in a surgery

| | | |
|---|---|---|
| 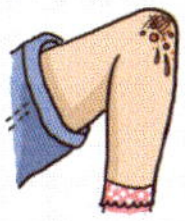 | **(to) bleed**<br>bluten | Sara fell, now her knee is bleeding. |
|  | **(to) cough**<br>husten | Tom is coughing loudly. |
|  | **(to) not feel well**<br>sich nicht gut fühlen | Mr Miller is not feeling well. |
|  | **(to) hear**<br>hören | Mrs Summer is old. She cannot hear well. |
|  | **(to) help**<br>helfen | Can I help you? |
|  | **(to) smell**<br>riechen | Do you smell anything? |
|   | **(to) sneeze**<br>niesen | Brian has got a cold. He is sneezing. |
|  | **(to) taste**<br>schmecken | Medicine normally doesn't taste good. |
|  | **(to) touch**<br>berühren | Don't touch the wound. |

## The head

| | | |
|---|---|---|
|  | **head**<br>der Kopf | The head is the upper part of the body. |
|  | **face**<br>das Gesicht | Tony has a very dirty face. |
|  | **hair**<br>die Haare | Sally has long brown hair. |
| 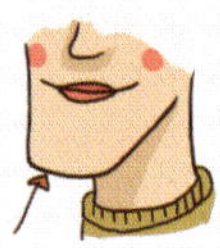 | **chin**<br>das Kinn | The chin is the part below the mouth. |
| 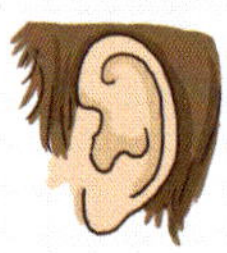 | **ear**<br>das Ohr | You hear with your ears. |
| 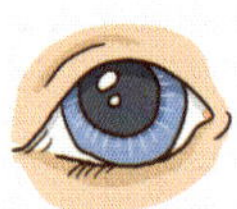 | **eye**<br>das Auge | You see with your eyes. |
| 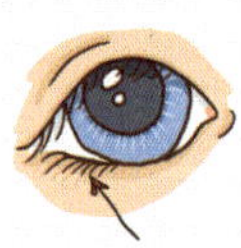 | **eye lashes**<br>die Wimpern | The eyelashes are around the eye. |
|  | **mouth**<br>der Mund | You eat with your mouth. |
|  | **nose**<br>die Nase | You smell with your nose. |
|  | **neck**<br>der Hals | Your head is on your neck. |

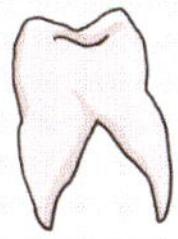

**tooth** — Ron lost a tooth.

der Zahn

**teeth** — The baby has got two teeth.

die Zähne

## The body

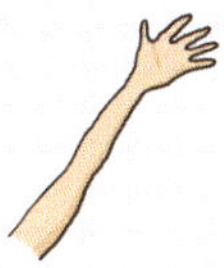

**arm** — You have two arms.

der Arm

**back** — Grandfather‘s back hurts.

der Rücken

**belly** — Tina is showing her belly.

der Bauch

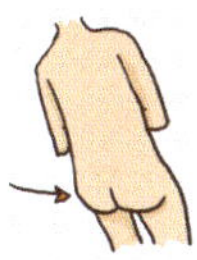

**bottom** — Your bottom is under your back.

der Po

**chest** — Stand straight and put out your chest.

die Brust

**elbow** — Ouch, I bumped my elbow.

der Ellbogen

## The body

| | | |
|---|---|---|
| 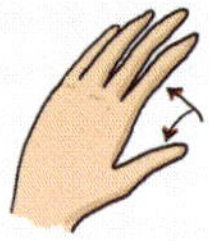 | **finger**<br>der Finger | You have five fingers on your hand. |
| 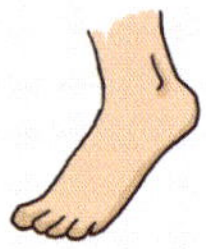 | **foot**<br>der Fuß | Can you stand on one foot? |
| 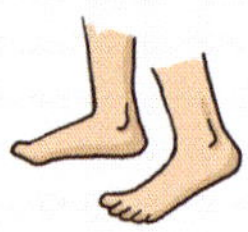 | **feet**<br>die Füße | You walk on your two feet. |
| 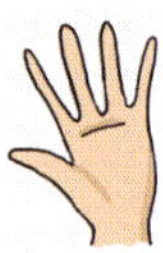 | **hand**<br>die Hand | Every person has two hands. |
| 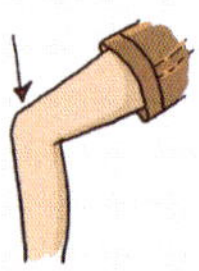 | **knee**<br>das Knie | Bend your knees, please. |
|  | **leg**<br>das Bein | You have two legs, a dog has four. |
|  | **shoulder**<br>die Schulter | The hamster is sitting on Lucy‘s shoulder. |
| 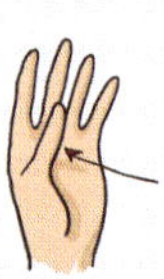 | **thumb**<br>der Daumen | The thumb is the short thick finger on your hand. |
| 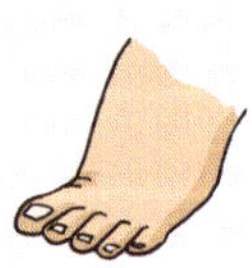 | **toe**<br>der Zeh | You have five toes on your foot. |
| 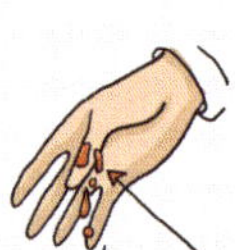 | **blood**<br>das Blut | I can‘t see blood. It makes me feel ill. |

## When you don't feel well

| | | |
|---|---|---|
|  | **broken arm**<br>der gebrochene Arm | Tim's arm is broken. He has got a plaster cast. |
|  | **bruise**<br>der blaue Fleck | Sandy has many bruises on her leg. |
|  | **cough**<br>der Husten | Mr Winter has a bad cough. |
|  | **headache**<br>die Kopfschmerzen | My head hurts. I have a headache. |
|  | **sore throat**<br>die Halsschmerzen | I cannot swallow. I have a sore throat. |
|  | **stomach ache**<br>die Bauchschmerzen | I ate something bad. I have a stomach ache. |
|  | **toothache**<br>die Zahnschmerzen | Mr Khan has a bad toothache. |
| 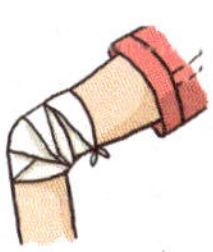 | **bandage**<br>der Verband | The doctor put a bandage on the wound. |
| 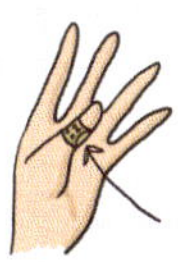 | **plaster**<br>das Pflaster | I cut my finger. I put a plaster around it. |

# Pets

| | | |
|---|---|---|
|  | **budgie**<br>der Wellensittich | Emma has got a green budgie. |
|  | **cat**<br>die Katze | The cat is black and white. |
|  | **dog**<br>der Hund | There are small dogs and big dogs. |
|  | **fish**<br>der Fisch | There are many fish in the fish tank. |
|  | **gerbil**<br>die Wüstenspringmaus | Gerbils are very active animals. |
|  | **goldfish**<br>der Goldfisch | Goldfish are very popular pets in Japan. |
|  | **guinea pig**<br>das Meerschweinchen | We have got four guinea pigs. |
|  | **hamster**<br>der Hamster | Hamsters sleep during the day. |
|  | **mouse**<br>die Maus | Some people are afraid of my little mouse. |
|  | **parrot**<br>der Papagei | Can your parrot talk? |

**rabbit**
das Kaninchen

Do you keep your rabbit inside or outside?

**spider**
die Spinne

Paul has got a big black spider for a pet.

**tortoise**
die Schildkröte

A tortoise is a very quiet pet.

## What you do with pets

**(to) examine**
untersuchen

The vet is examining the dog.

**(to) feed**
füttern

You must feed your dog twice a day.

**(to) give an injection**
eine Spritze geben

The vet is giving the dog an injection.

**(to) pet**
streicheln

I like to pet my dog. He also likes it.

**(to) take care of**
sich kümmern um

Please take care of your dog.

## Body parts of a pet

| | | |
|---|---|---|
|  | **beak**<br>der Schnabel | A bird has a beak, not a mouth. |
|  | **claw**<br>die Kralle | A cat has sharp claws. |
|  | **ear**<br>das Ohr | This dog has long ears. |
|  | **eye**<br>das Auge | Our dog has black eyes. |
|  | **fur**<br>das Fell | The dog‘s fur is very shiny. |
| 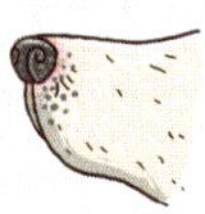 | **mouth**<br>die Schnauze | Don‘t touch the dog‘s mouth. |
|  | **paw**<br>die Pfote | Tessa‘s dog is black, but has a brown paw. |
|  | **tail**<br>der Schwanz | The dog is wagging its tail happily. |
|  | **whiskers**<br>die Barthaare | A cat has sensitive whiskers. |
|  | **wing**<br>der Flügel | A bird uses its wings to fly. |

## What pets can do

| | | |
|---|---|---|
|  | **(to) bark**<br>bellen | Dogs bark. |
|  | **(to) bite**<br>beißen | Some dogs bite – watch out. |
|  | **(to) drink**<br>trinken | Not only people, also pets have to drink. |
|  | **(to) eat**<br>fressen | Tim‘s rabbit likes to eat carrots. |
|  | **(to) fly**<br>fliegen | My budgie likes to fly around in my bedroom. |
|  | **(to) jump**<br>springen | Can your rabbit jump up high? |
|  | **(to) run**<br>rennen | Sally‘s dog can run very fast. |
|  | **(to) scratch**<br>kratzen | Oh no! The cat is scratching the sofa again. |
|  | **(to) swim**<br>schwimmen | Goldfish don‘t like to swim in circles. |

# Sports and hobbies

# What you do in your leisure time

| | | |
|---|---|---|
|  | **(to) collect**<br>sammeln | Do you collect anything? |
|  | **(to) collect stickers**<br>Aufkleber sammeln | I collect stickers. I've got a sticker album. |
|  | **(to) dance**<br>tanzen | I like to dance. And you? |
|  | **(to) do ballet**<br>Ballett machen | Mandy is doing ballet. |
|  | **(to) ice-skate**<br>eislaufen | In winter Lisa ice-skates on frozen lakes. |
|  | **(to) meet friends**<br>Freunde treffen | I like to meet my friends every day. |
|  | **(to) play chess**<br>Schach spielen | My hobby is playing chess. |
|  | **(to) play football**<br>Fußball spielen | Tim is playing football in a football team. |
| 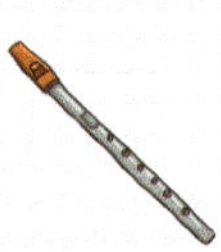 | **(to) play the recorder**<br>Flöte spielen | John is playing the recorder. |
|  | **(to) read**<br>lesen | Kalim's favourite hobby is reading. |

**(to) ride a bike** — Linus likes to ride his bike.

Rad fahren

**(to) ride a horse** — Ali doesn‘t want to ride a horse.

reiten

**(to) paint** — I can‘t paint well.

malen

**(to) sing** — I like singing. I sing in a choir at school.

singen

**(to) skate** — During the summer I skate a lot.

skaten

## Do you like it?

**It's fun.** — I like to read comics. It‘s fun!

Es macht Spaß.

**It's boring.** — I don‘t like to draw pictures. It‘s boring.

Es ist langweilig.

**It's exciting.** — Meeting new friends is exciting.

Es ist aufregend.

## Sports

**athletics**
Leichtathletik

I'm good at athletics.

**badminton**
Badminton

You need two rackets to play badminton.

**baseball**
Baseball

Baseball is very popular in America.

**basketball**
Basketball

To play basketball you have to be tall.

**football**
Fußball

Football is the biggest sport in Germany.

**golf**
Golf

Golf is becoming more and more popular.

**gymnastics**
Gymnastik

Not many boys like to do gymnastics.

**hockey**
Hockey

For hockey you need hockey sticks and a ball.

**ice hockey**
Eishockey

You play ice hockey in an ice rink.

**horseback riding**
Reiten

Horseback riding is an expensive sport.

**judo**
Judo

Michael's favourite sport is judo.

**running**
Laufen

For running you need good shoes.

**sailing**
Segeln

For sailing you need a lake or the sea nearby.

**skiing**
Skifahren

In winter you can go skiing.

**swimming**
Schwimmen

Swimming is very exciting to watch.

**table tennis**
Tischtennis

We play table tennis at home.

**tennis**
Tennis

My parents like to play tennis.

**volleyball**
Volleyball

Volleyball is a team sport.

**windsurfing**
Windsurfen

It has to be windy to do windsurfing.

## The game is on

| | | |
|---|---|---|
|  | **champion**<br>der Champion | Tim won every time. He‘s the champion. |
|  | **coach**<br>der Trainer | The coach is shouting out loud. |
|  | **game**<br>das Spiel | In football you call a game a „match“. |
|  | **loser**<br>der Verlierer | Simon is sad. He is the loser of the game. |
|  | **player**<br>der Spieler | The players are singing the national anthem. |
| 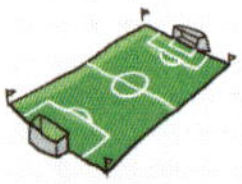 | **playing field**<br>das Spielfeld | The playing field was too wet to play on. |
|  | **race**<br>das Rennen | The car race in Monaco is famous. |
|  | **referee**<br>der Schiedsrichter | The referee was very fair. |
|  | **team**<br>die Mannschaft | There are 11 players in each football team. |
|  | **winner**<br>der Sieger | The winner got a new car. |

## How you feel doing sports

| | | |
|---|---|---|
|  | **happy**<br>glücklich | I won the match. I'm very happy. |
|  | **sad**<br>traurig | You lost the match. You're sad. |
|  | **angry**<br>wütend | The referee was wrong, the players are angry. |
|  | **fast**<br>schnell | You can run very fast. |
|  | **slow**<br>langsam | In this race I was very slow. I lost it. |
|  | **better**<br>besser | In the next race I will win. I can do it better. |
|  | **as good as**<br>so gut wie | In swimming I'm as good as my friend. |
|  | **first**<br>erster | Michael did a great race. He was first. |
|  | **last**<br>letzter | Tom's race was not good today.<br>He came in last. |

## At the zoo

## At the zoo

| | | |
|---|---|---|
|  | **compound**<br>das Gehege | In modern zoos the compounds are very big. |
|  | **feeding time**<br>die Fütterung | Feeding time for the lions is at 2 o'clock. |
|  | **fence**<br>der Zaun | There's a fence around each compound. |
|   | **gate**<br>das Tor | There's a big gate at the entrance of the zoo. |
|  | **path**<br>der Weg | There's a path between the compounds. |
|  | **petting zoo**<br>der Streichelzoo | Children like to go to the petting zoo. |
|  | **pool**<br>das Becken | The seals are swimming around in the pool. |
|  | **showtime**<br>die Vorführung | Some zoos offer showtimes. |
|  | **sign**<br>das Schild | Follow the signs, then you won't get lost. |
|   | **ticket**<br>die Eintrittskarte | You need a ticket to get into the zoo. |

**ticket office**
der Kartenschalter

You can buy your ticket at the ticket office.

**ticket officer**
der Kartenverkäufer

The ticket officer is selling tickets.

**visitor**
der Besucher

Every day many visitors go to the zoo.

**zoo keeper**
der Tierpfleger

The zoo keeper takes care of the animals.

## What you do or not do in a zoo

**(to) climb**
klettern

Do not climb the fence.

**(to) look at**
ansehen

At the zoo you can look at wild animals.

**(to) throw**
werfen

Do not throw anything into the compounds.

**(to) visit**
besuchen

You can visit different shows.

## Wild animals

**bear**
der Bär
A bear looks friendly, but it is a wild animal.

**crocodile**
das Krokodil
Crocodiles are very dangerous animals.

**deer**
der Hirsch
A deer is a very shy animal.

**dolphin**
der Delfin
The dolphin jumps out of the water.

**elephant**
der Elefant
The elephant is a very big animal.

**giraffe**
die Giraffe
Giraffes have a long neck.

**hippo**
das Nilpferd
The hippo is standing in the water.

**kangaroo**
das Känguruh
The kangaroos jump around.

**lion**
der Löwe
The lion is looking for some food.

**lizard**
die Eidechse
The lizard is lying in the sun.

| | | |
|---|---|---|
|  | **panda**<br>der Panda | The panda eats bamboo leaves. |
|  | **parrot**<br>der Papagei | Parrots are very colourful. |
|  | **peacock**<br>der Pfau | The peacock is fanning out its tail. |
|  | **penguin**<br>der Pinguin | Penguins look funny. |
|  | **polar bear**<br>der Eisbär | The polar bear is diving for fish. |
|  | **seal**<br>der Seehund | Seals are living in the sea. |
|  | **snake**<br>die Schlange | The snake is not moving at all. |
|  | **tiger**<br>der Tiger | The tiger looks very hungry. |
|  | **wolf**<br>der Wolf | Wolves can howl very loud. |

## On the playground

| | | |
|---|---|---|
|  | **ball**<br>der Ball | Many children like to play ball. |
|  | **bench**<br>die Bank | There is a green bench in the park. |
| 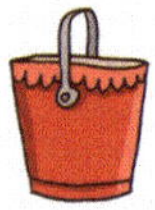 | **bucket**<br>der Eimer | The bucket is red. |
|  | **buggy**<br>der Buggy | The buggy is standing next to the bench. |
|  | **climbing frame**<br>das Klettergerüst | Tessa likes climbing on the climbing frame. |
|  | **doll**<br>die Puppe | Many children have got a doll at home. |
|  | **hopscotch**<br>das Hüpfspiel | Do you know hopscotch? |
|  | **kite**<br>der Drachen | Look at the blue kite in the sky! |
|  | **picnic rug**<br>die Picknickdecke | After the picnic, the picnic rug is very dirty. |
| 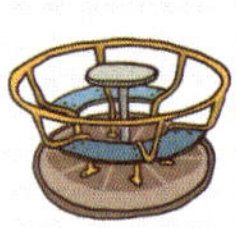 | **roundabout**<br>das Karussell | I don't like to go fast on the roundabout. |

**sand castle**
die Sandburg

Who wants to build a sand castle for Ron?

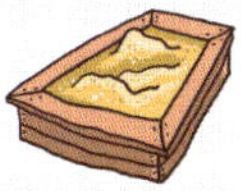

**sandbox**
die Sandkiste

Little children play in the sandbox.

**see-saw**
die Wippe

The see-saw is for four children.

**skipping rope**
das Springseil

I cannot skip. I haven't got a skipping rope.

**spade**
die Schaufel

You need a spade to build a sand castle.

**swing**
die Schaukel

Can you push me on the swing, please?

**slide**
die Rutsche

This is a small slide for little children.

**teddy bear**
der Teddy

This teddy bear is wearing a scarf.

**toy car**
das Spielzeugauto

Do you like this blue toy car?

# Down at the farm

# On the farm

**barn** — die Scheune — You keep straw in the barn.

**dunghill** — der Misthaufen — The dunghill is very smelly.

**farmhouse** — das Bauernhaus — The farmhouse is next to the barn.

**kennel** — die Hundehütte — A kennel is for the dog to sleep in.

**pigsty** — der Schweinestall — There are many pigs in the pigsty.

**rabbit hutch** — der Kaninchenstall — We keep our rabbits in a rabbit hutch.

**scarecrow** — die Vogelscheuche — A scarecrow is made of straw.

**stable** — der Stall — The animals are in the stable.

**vegetable patch** — das Gemüsebeet — In the vegetable patch grow carrots.

**(to) watch** — bewachen — The dog is watching the farm.

## What a farmer does

| | | |
|---|---|---|
|  | **(to) clear out**<br>ausmisten | The farmer is clearing out the cowshed. |
|  | **(to) collect**<br>sammeln | The farmer collects the eggs in the morning. |
|  | **(to) feed**<br>füttern | The farmer is feeding the cows. |
|  | **(to) harvest**<br>ernten | In the autumn you can harvest many things. |
|  | **(to) milk**<br>melken | You have to milk the cows every day. |
|  | **(to) pick**<br>pflücken | The farmer‘s wife is picking apples. |
|  | **(to) plant**<br>pflanzen | John has planted a tree. |
|  | **(to) repair**<br>reparieren | The tractor is broken. The farmer must repair it. |
|  | **(to) ride a horse**<br>reiten | Brian is riding a pony. |

## Farm animals

**cat**
die Katze

On many farms you can find a cat.

**calf**
das Kalb

The baby of a cow is called a calf.

**chick**
das Küken

The baby of a hen is called a chick.

**cock**
der Hahn

The cock crows early in the morning.

**cow**
die Kuh

A cow gives milk.

**dog**
der Hund

The dog is barking.

**donkey**
der Esel

A donkey is grey.

**duck**
die Ente

There are many ducks swimming on the pond.

**goat**
die Ziege

A goat gives milk. Have you tried goat cheese?

**hen**
das Huhn

Hens lay eggs.

**goose**
die Gans

A goose is white.

**geese**
die Gänse

Geese can be very aggressive.

**horse**
das Pferd

You can ride on a horse.

**lamb**
das Lamm

The baby of a sheep is called a lamb.

**mouse**
die Maus

The mouse is running away from the cat.

**mice**
die Mäuse

On a farm there are many mice.

**pig**
das Schwein

Pigs like to lie in the mud.

**piglet**
das Ferkel

The baby of a pig is called a piglet.

**sheep**
das Schaf

Sheep give wool.

## Nature

| | | |
|---|---|---|
|  | **bush**<br>der Busch | There are some bushes in the field. |
|  | **cloud**<br>die Wolke | There's a big cloud in the sky. |
|  | **flower**<br>die Blume | My favourite flower is the rose. |
|  | **forest**<br>der Wald | It's dark in the forest. |
|  | **grass**<br>das Gras | Nothing grows here but grass. |
| 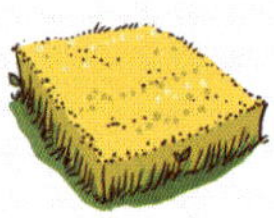 | **field**<br>das Feld | A field of ripe wheat is yellow. |
| 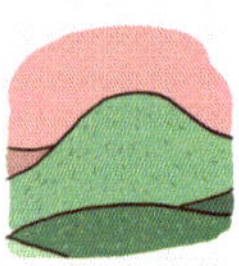 | **hill**<br>der Hügel | From that hill you have got a great view. |
|  | **lake**<br>der See | Let's go swimming in the lake! |
|  | **leaf**<br>das Blatt | A leaf can be green, red, orange or brown. |
|  | **leaves**<br>die Blätter | There are many leaves on a tree. |

**meadow**

die Wiese

In the meadow there are many flowers.

**pond**

der Teich

A pond is a small lake.

**puddle**

die Pfütze

After it has rained, there are many puddles.

**rain**

der Regen

We need some rain, it's very dry.

**rainbow**

der Regenbogen

Do you know the colours of the rainbow?

**river**

der Fluss

The river Thames runs through London.

**sky**

der Himmel

The sky is blue today.

**sun**

die Sonne

During the day the sun is shining.

**tree**

der Baum

I like trees, and you?

# In town

Welcome
Bakery
fresh
OPEN
BUS
STOP

# In town

| | | |
|---|---|---|
|  | **bench**<br>die Bank | Let's sit down on the bench. |
|  | **block of flats**<br>das Mehrfamilienhaus | I live in this block of flats. |
|  | **bridge**<br>die Brücke | The bridge is made of stone. |
|  | **building**<br>das Gebäude | There are many new buildings in town. |
|  | **city**<br>die (Innen)Stadt | You find a lot of banks in the city. |
|  | **cycle lane**<br>der Fahrradweg | Use the cycle lane when you ride your bike. |
|  | **cyclist**<br>der Radfahrer | The cyclist is riding his bike very fast. |
|  | **driver**<br>der Fahrer | The taxi driver is very friendly. |
|  | **flat**<br>die Wohnung | Our flat has got three bedrooms. |
|  | **fountain**<br>der Brunnen | The water in the fountain is dirty. |

| | | |
|---|---|---|
|  | **house**<br>das Haus | We live in the yellow house. |
|  | **junction**<br>die Kreuzung | There's an accident at the junction. |
|  | **letterbox**<br>der Briefkasten | Please put this letter in the letterbox. |
|  | **pedestrian**<br>der Fußgänger | A pedestrian is a person that is going on foot. |
|   | **pedestrian zone**<br>die Fußgängerzone | No cars are allowed in the pedestrian zone. |
|  | **pavement**<br>der Bürgersteig | Pedestrians walk on the pavement. |
|  | **street light**<br>die Straßenlaterne | The street lights are off. It's very dark. |
|   | **street sign**<br>das Straßenschild | Can you read the street sign?<br>– Yes, High Street. |
|   | **traffic sign**<br>das Verkehrsschild | Traffic signs show you what to do in traffic. |

## In town

**traffic light**
die Ampel

When the traffic light is red, you must stop.

**town**
die Stadt

Do you live in a big town?

**village**
das Dorf

A village is smaller than a town.

**zebra crossing**
der Zebrastreifen

Cars must stop at a zebra crossing.

## Directions

**left**
links

Turn left at the town hall.

**on the left**
auf der linken Seite

The school is on the left.

**right**
rechts

Turn right at the supermarket.

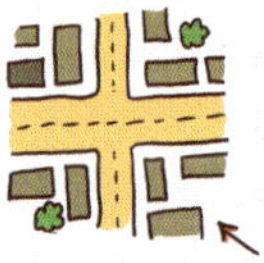

**on the right**
auf der rechten Seite

The swimming pool is on the right.

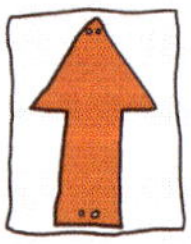

**straight ahead**
geradeaus

Walk straight ahead.

## What you do in town

| | | |
|---|---|---|
|  | **(to) buy a ticket**<br>eine Fahrkarte kaufen | I must buy a ticket for the bus. |
|  | **(to) go by …**<br>mit etwas fahren | I will go by train. |
|  | **(to) ride a bike**<br>Rad fahren | I ride my bike every day. |
|  | **(to) walk**<br>gehen | We can walk, the museum is not far away. |
|  | **(to) get on**<br>einsteigen | Quick – get on the bus! It's leaving soon. |
|  | **(to) get off**<br>aussteigen | We must get off the bus at the next stop. |
|  | **(to) queue**<br>sich anstellen | In England you always queue at the bus stop. |
|  | **(to) go sightseeing**<br>Sehenswürdigkeiten ansehen | I like to go sightseeing. |
|  | **(to) live**<br>leben | Where do you live?<br>– In Germany. |

## Buildings

**bakery**
die Bäckerei

You can buy bread at a bakery.

**bank**
die Bank

At a bank you can change money.

**pharmacy**
die Apotheke

You can get medicine at the pharmacy.

**church**
die Kirche

Many people go to church on Sundays.

**cinema**
das Kino

Let's go to the cinema and watch the new film.

**factory**
die Fabrik

Many people work in factories.

**hospital**
das Krankenhaus

The ambulance is going to the hospital.

**hotel**
das Hotel

On our holidays, we stay in a hotel.

**library**
die Bücherei

In a library you find many books and CDs.

**office building**
das Bürogebäude

There's a new office building next to the park.

| | | |
|---|---|---|
|  | **petrol station**<br>die Tankstelle | At the petrol station you get petrol for cars. |
|  | **post office**<br>die Post | You buy stamps at the post office. |
|  | **train station**<br>der Bahnhof | There are many people at the train station. |
|  | **restaurant**<br>das Restaurant | Do you like to eat in restaurants? |
|  | **school**<br>die Schule | The school I go to is very old. |
|  | **shop**<br>das Geschäft | There is a shop right next to our house. |
|  | **stadium**<br>das Stadion | I would like to watch a match in the stadium. |
|  | **supermarket**<br>der Supermarkt | Every Friday we go to the supermarket to buy groceries. |
|  | **swimming pool**<br>das Schwimmbad | There's an indoor swimming pool in town. |

## Vehicles

| | | | |
|---|---|---|---|
| 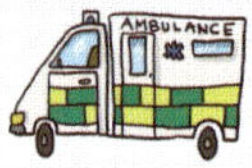 | **ambulance** | der Krankenwagen | The ambulance takes ill people to the hospital. |
|  | **bike** | das Fahrrad | Please wear a helmet when you ride your bike. |
|  | **boat** | das Boot | Let's row the boat across the river. |
|  | **bus** | der Bus | At the bus stop you wait for the bus. |
|  | **car** | das Auto | My father goes to work by car. |
|  | **caravan** | das Wohnmobil | We spent our holidays in a caravan. |
|  | **fire engine** | das Feuerwehrauto | It's burning – the fire engine is coming fast. |
|  | **helicopter** | der Hubschrauber | The helicopter is flying across the city. |
|  | **inline skates** | die Inliner | Kim got new inline skates for her birthday. |
|  | **lorry** | der Lastwagen | A lorry can transport many things. |

| | | |
|---|---|---|
|  | **motorbike**<br>das Motorrad | Brian hasn‘t got a car. He has got a motorbike. |
|  | **plane**<br>das Flugzeug | You can see many planes at the airport. |
|  | **police car**<br>das Polizeiauto | There are two policemen in the police car. |
|  | **scooter**<br>der Roller | Many children like to use their scooters. |
|  | **ship**<br>das Schiff | You can see big ships in the harbour. |
|  | **taxi**<br>das Taxi | Let‘s take a taxi. |
|  | **train**<br>der Zug | There are many passengers on the train. |
|  | **tram**<br>die Straßenbahn | Is there a tram in your town? |
|  | **underground**<br>die U-Bahn | The underground in London is called “the tube”. |

## People and jobs

**people**

die Menschen

About 8 million people live in London.

**boy**

der Junge

Tom is a boy.

**girl**

das Mädchen

Tessa is a girl.

**child**

das Kind

Sam is an only child.

**children**

die Kinder

Many children have brothers or sisters.

**man**

der Mann

A male person is called a man.

**woman**

die Frau

A female person is called a woman.

**baker**

der Bäcker

A baker bakes bread and cakes.

**builder**

der Bauarbeiter

You need many builders to build a house.

**bus driver**

der Busfahrer

A bus driver is driving a bus.

| | | |
|---|---|---|
|  | **cook**<br>der Koch | A cook cooks the meals in a restaurant. |
|  | **firefighter**<br>der Feuerwehrmann | To be a firefighter is a dangerous job. |
|  | **hairdresser**<br>die Friseurin | The hairdresser is cutting your hair. |
|  | **policeman**<br>der Polizist | Some policemen control the traffic. |
|  | **policewoman**<br>die Polizistin | Some policewomen catch thieves. |
|  | **postman**<br>der Briefträger | The postman brings the letters and postcards. |
|  | **teacher**<br>die Lehrerin | What's the name of your Maths teacher? |
|  | **waiter**<br>der Kellner | Waiters and waitresses work in restaurants. |
|  | **waitress**<br>die Kellnerin | The waitress serves the meals at your table. |

## All year round

JUN
JUL
AUG
+30
0
-0
-10
SEP
OCT
NOV
DEC

## The seasons and the months

**calendar**
der Kalender

The calendar shows the 12 months of the year.

**season**
die Jahreszeit

There are four seasons in a year.

**spring**
der Frühling

Spring starts in March.

**summer**
der Sommer

My favourite season is summer.

**autumn**
der Herbst

In autumn the leaves are falling from the trees.

**winter**
der Winter

In winter we sometimes have snow.

**month**
der Monat

There are 12 months in a year.

**January**
Januar

January is the 1st month of the year.

**February**
Februar

February is the 2nd month of the year.

**March**
März

March is the 3rd month of the year.

**April**
April

April is the 4th month of the year.

**May**
Mai

May is the 5th month of the year.

**June**
Juni

June is the 6th month of the year.

**July**
Juli

July is the 7th month of the year.

**August**
August

August is the 8th month of the year.

**September**
September

September is the 9th month of the year.

**October**
Oktober

October is the 10th month of the year.

**November**
November

November is the 11th month of the year.

**December**
Dezember

December is the 12th month of the year.

## The week

**week**
die Woche

The week has seven days.

**weekend**
das Wochenende

Saturday and Sunday are the weekend.

**day**
der Tag

A day has 24 hours.

**Monday**
Montag

On Monday I play tennis.

**Tuesday**
Dienstag

On Tuesday I go to ballet.

**Wednesday**
Mittwoch

On Wednesday I play the piano.

**Thursday**
Donnerstag

On Thursday I must go to the dentist.

**Friday**
Freitag

On Friday I visit my grandparents.

**Saturday**
Samstag

On Saturday we go shopping.

**Sunday**
Sonntag

On Sunday we go for a walk in the park.

**in the morning**
am Morgen

Can you hear the birds in the morning?

**in the afternoon**
am Nachmittag

In the afternoon I play with my friends.

**in the evening**
am Abend

In the evening I go to bed.

**at night**
in der Nacht

At night I sleep.

**noon**
Mittag

The sun is at its highest at noon.

**at midnight**
um Mitternacht

At midnight the bell strikes 12 times.

**early**
früh

I don‘t like to get up early.

**late**
spät

I like to go to bed late.

**at … o’clock**
um … Uhr

We have dinner at 6 o‘clock.

## When?

| | | |
|---|---|---|
|  | **yesterday**<br>gestern | Yesterday I was in London. |
|  | **today**<br>heute | Today I am in Hamburg. |
|  | **tomorrow**<br>morgen | Tomorrow I will be in Paris. |

## Easter

| | | |
|---|---|---|
|  | **daffodil**<br>die Osterglocke | England is famous for its many daffodils. |
|  | **Easter basket**<br>der Osterkorb | You collect the eggs into the Easter basket. |
|  | **Easter bunny**<br>der Osterhase | Do you believe in the Easter bunny? |
|  | **Easter egg**<br>das Osterei | Many Easter eggs are made of chocolate. |
|  | **nest**<br>das Nest | There are three pink Easter eggs in the nest. |
|  | **tulip**<br>die Tulpe | I like tulips very much. |

# Halloween

| | | |
|---|---|---|
|  | **bat**<br>die Fledermaus | The bats are coming out when it is getting dark. |
|  | **ghost**<br>der Geist | Do you believe in ghosts? |
|  | **Halloween**<br>Halloween | Halloween is on 31st October. |
|  | **pumpkin**<br>der Kürbis | You can cut funny faces into a pumpkin. |
|  | **spider**<br>die Spinne | Are you afraid of spiders? |
|  | **treat**<br>die Süßigkeit | Trick or treat? Give us something nice to eat! |
|  | **trick**<br>der Streich | Don‘t play any bad trick on me, please. |
|  | **witch**<br>die Hexe | Emma has dressed up as a witch. |
|  | **mummy**<br>die Mumie | Nick has dressed up as a mummy. |

## The weather

**cloud**
die Wolke

There is one big cloud in the sky.

**cloudy**
wolkig

Today it is very cloudy.

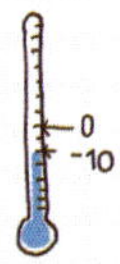


**cold**
kalt

It is a cold day.

**dry**
trocken

I am happy that it is a dry day today.

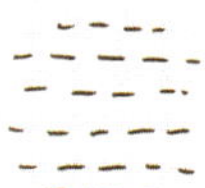

**fog**
der Nebel

In November there is a lot of fog.

**foggy**
neblig

Yesterday it was very foggy.

**grey**
grau

What a grey day!

**hot**
heiß

In summer it can be very hot.

**rain**
der Regen

I don't like the rain.

**rainbow**
der Regenbogen

Have you seen the rainbow?

**rainy** — regnerisch — It's rainy.

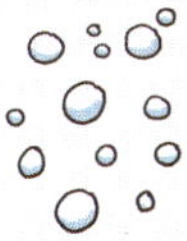

**snow** — der Schnee — The children are waiting for the snow.

**storm** — der Sturm — There is a big storm coming.

**sun** — die Sonne — There wasn't much sun last week.

**sunny** — sonnig — Tomorrow it's going to be sunny again.

**warm** — warm — It's nice and warm today.

**wet** — nass — It rained a lot. Now everything is wet.

**wind** — der Wind — There is no wind today.

**windy** — windig — Yesterday it was very windy.

## Numbers

| | | |
|---|---|---|
| 1 | **one**<br>eins | Would you like one scoop of ice cream or two? |
| 2 | **two**<br>zwei | I have got two sisters. |
| 3 | **three**<br>drei | The cat has got three kittens. |
| 4 | **four**<br>vier | A clover with four leaves means luck. |
| 5 | **five**<br>fünf | There are five chocolates left. |
| 6 | **six**<br>sechs | To start the game you have to throw a six. |
| 7 | **seven**<br>sieben | Seven is a magic number in fairy tales. |
| 8 | **eight**<br>acht | Look at the eight birds on the roof! |
| 9 | **nine**<br>neun | School starts at nine. |
| 10 | **ten**<br>zehn | We are ten friends. |

## Colours

| | | | |
|---|---|---|---|
|  | **black** | schwarz | Black is a very dark colour. |
|  | **blue** | blau | The sky is blue. |
|  | **brown** | braun | Peter's jacket is brown. |
|  | **green** | grün | Grass is green. |
|  | **orange** | orange | My favourite colour is orange. |
|  | **purple** | lila | You can buy green grapes and purple grapes. |
|  | **red** | rot | Do you like red? |
|  | **yellow** | gelb | Bananas are yellow. |
|  | **white** | weiß | When you mix black and white you get grey. |

## Numbers

| | | |
|---|---|---|
| 11 | **eleven**<br>elf | 11 minus 1 is 10. |
| 12 | **twelve**<br>zwölf | 12 minus 1 is 11. |
| 13 | **thirteen**<br>dreizehn | 13 minus 1 is 12. |
| 14 | **fourteen**<br>vierzehn | 14 minus 1 is 13. |
| 15 | **fifteen**<br>fünfzehn | 15 minus 1 is 14. |
| 16 | **sixteen**<br>sechzehn | 16 minus 1 is 15. |
| 17 | **seventeen**<br>siebzehn | 17 minus 1 is 16. |
| 18 | **eighteen**<br>achtzehn | 18 minus 1 is 17. |
| 19 | **nineteen**<br>neunzehn | 19 minus 1 is 18. |
| 20 | **twenty**<br>zwanzig | 20 minus 1 is 19. |

| | | |
|---|---|---|
| 30 | **thirty**<br>dreißig | 30 plus 10 is 40. |
| 40 | **forty**<br>vierzig | 40 plus 10 is 50. |
| 50 | **fifty**<br>fünfzig | 50 plus 10 is 60. |
| 60 | **sixty**<br>sechzig | 60 plus 10 is 70. |
| 70 | **seventy**<br>siebzig | 70 plus 10 is 80. |
| 80 | **eighty**<br>achtzig | 80 plus 10 is 90. |
| 90 | **ninety**<br>neunzig | 90 plus 10 is 100. |
| 100 | **one hundred**<br>hundert | 100 plus 10 is 110. |
| 1000 | **one thousand**<br>tausend | 1000 plus 1000 is 2000. |

## Ordinal numbers

**1st (first)**
der Erste

**2nd (second)**
der Zweite

**3rd (third)**
der Dritte

**4th (fourth)**
der Vierte

**5th (fifth)**
der Fünfte

**6th (sixth)**
der Sechste

**7th (seventh)**
der Siebte

**8th (eighth)**
der Achte

**9th (ninth)**
der Neunte

**10th (tenth)**
der Zehnte

## Mathematical expressions

**plus**
plus

**divided by**
geteilt durch

**more**
mehr

**is**
ist gleich

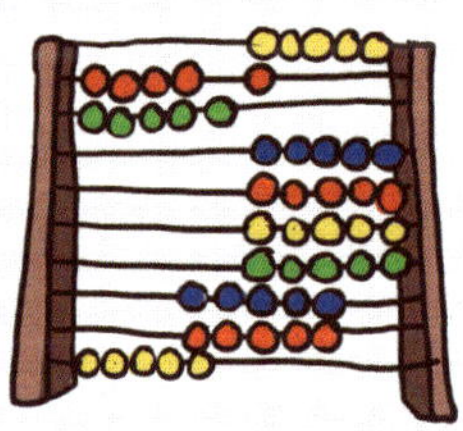

**minus**
minus

**multiplied with**
mal

**less**
weniger

## Shapes

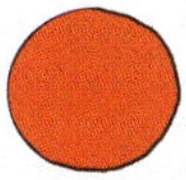

**circle**

der Kreis

The circle is round and red.

**cross**

das Kreuz

The cross is orange.

**cylinder**

der Zylinder

The cylinder is brown.

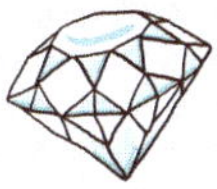

**diamond**

der Diamant

The diamond is white.

**heart**

das Herz

The heart is pink.

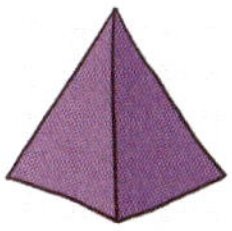

**pyramid**

die Pyramide

The pyramid is purple.

**rectangle**

das Rechteck

The rectangle is blue.

**square**

das Quadrat

The square is green.

**triangle**

das Dreieck

The triangle is yellow.

## The personal pronouns

| | | | | | |
|---|---|---|---|---|---|
| **I** | ich | **me** | mir | **my** | mein |
| **you** | du | **you** | dir | **your** | dein |
| **he** | er | **him** | ihm | **his** | sein |
| **she** | sie | **her** | ihr | **her** | ihr |
| **it** | es | **it** | ihm | **its** | sein |
| **we** | wir | **us** | uns | **our** | unser |
| **you** | ihr | **you** | euch | **your** | euer |
| **they** | sie | **them** | ihnen | **their** | ihr |

## The forms of to be

**I am**
ich bin

I am a girl.

**you are**
du bist

You are a boy.

**he, she, it is**
er, sie, es ist

He is tall.

**we are**
wir sind

We are friends.

**you are**
ihr seid

You are new in town.

**they are**
sie sind

They are very friendly.

## Is it ...?

**Is it okay for you?**
Ist es in Ordnung für dich?

**Yes, it is.**
Ja, ist es.

**Is it okay for you?**
Ist es in Ordnung für Sie?

**No, it isn't.**
Nein, ist es nicht.

## The forms of to have (got)

| | |
|---|---|
| **I have got**<br>ich habe | I have got a brother. |
| **you have got**<br>du hast | You have got a sister. |
| **he, she, it has got**<br>er, sie, es hat | He has got a dog. |
| **we have got**<br>wir haben | We have got many hobbies. |
| **you have got**<br>ihr habt | You have got a fast car. |
| **they have got**<br>sie haben | They have got four children. |

## Have you got ...?

**Have you got a pet?**

Hast du ein Haustier?

**Yes, I have.**

Ja, habe ich.

**Have you got a pet?**

Haben Sie ein Haustier?

**No, I haven't.**

Nein, habe ich nicht.

## The forms of can

| | |
|---|---|
| **I can**<br>ich kann | I can play football. |
| **you can**<br>du kannst | You can play tennis. |
| **he, she, it can**<br>er, sie, es kann | He can paint. |
| **we can**<br>wir können | We can sing. |
| **you can**<br>ihr könnt | You can play chess. |
| **they can**<br>sie können | They can swim. |

## Can you ...?

**Can you dance?**

Kannst du tanzen?

**Yes, I can.**

Ja, kann ich.

**Can you dance?**

Können Sie tanzen?

**No, I can't.**

Nein, kann ich nicht.

## Question words

**What?**
Was?

What are you doing?

**Who?**
Wer?

Who is this man? – Our new teacher.

**When?**
Wann?

When is your birthday? – In April.

**Where?**
Wo?

Where do you live? – In London.

**How many?**
Wie viele?

How many fingers are on a hand? – Five.

**How much?**
Wie viel?

How much is the ice cream? – 75 cents.

**Why?**
Warum?

Why are you late?
The bus was late.

**Which?**
Welche?

Which of the bikes is yours?
The green one.

# Glossar Englisch-Deutsch

## A

**address** die Adresse **20**
**aisle** der Gang **45**
**alarm clock** der Wecker **13**
**am** bin **9**
**ambulance** der Krankenwagen **100**
**angel** der Engel **113**
**angry** wütend **73**
**anorak** der Anorak **35**
**(to) answer** antworten **30**
**apple** der Apfel **47**
**April** April **107**
**are** sind **9**
**arm** der Arm **59**
**armchair** der Sessel **14**
**Art** Kunst **25**
**as good as** so gut wie **73**
**(to) ask** fragen **30**
**athletics** Leichtathletik **70**
**at home** zu Hause **20**
**at midnight** um Mitternacht **109**
**at night** in der Nacht **109**
**at ... o'clock** um ... Uhr **109**
**attic** der Dachboden **10**
**August** August **107**
**aunt** die Tante **9**
**autumn** der Herbst **106**

## B

**baby** das Baby **8**
**back** der Rücken **59**
**badminton** Badminton **70**
**bag** die Tasche **38**
**baker** der Bäcker **102**
**bakery** die Bäckerei **98**
**ball** der Ball **82**
**balloon** der Luftballon **112**
**banana** die Banane **47**
**bandage** der Verband **61**
**bank** die Bank **98**
**(to) bark** bellen **65**
**barn** die Scheune **86**
**baseball** Baseball **70**
**basin** das Waschbecken **14**
**basketball** Basketball **70**
**bat** die Fledermaus **111**
**bathing suit** der Badeanzug **35**
**bathroom** das Badezimmer **10**
**bathtub** die Badewanne **14**
**beak** der Schnabel **64**
**beans** die Bohnen **48**
**bear** der Bär **78**
**bed** das Bett **13**
**bedroom** das Schlafzimmer **10**
**behind** hinter **18**
**belly** der Bauch **59**
**belt** der Gürtel **35**
**bench** die Bank **82, 94**
**better** besser **73**
**between** zwischen **18**
**big** groß **80**
**bike** das Fahrrad **100**
**bikini** der Bikini **35**
**bin** der Papierkorb **27**
**bird house** das Vogelhaus **21**
**birthday** der Geburtstag **112**
**birthday cake** der Geburtstagskuchen **112**
**birthday card** die Geburtstagskarte **112**
**birthday party** die Geburtstagsparty **112**
**biscuit** der Keks **50**
**(to) bite** beißen **65**
**black** schwarz **117**
**blackboard** die Tafel **27**
**blanket** die Decke **13**
**(to) bleed** bluten **57**
**block of flats** das Mehrfamilienhaus **94**
**blood** das Blut **60**
**blouse** die Bluse **35**
**blue** blau **117**
**board** die Tafel **29**
**boat** das Boot **100**
**book** das Buch **27**
**bookcase** das Bücherregal **14**
**(a pair of) boots** die Stiefel **38**
**bottle** die Flasche **45**
**bottom** der Po **59**
**boy** der Junge **24, 102**
**bracelet** das Armband **39**
**bread** das Brot **50**
**breaktime** die Pause **25**
**bridge** die Brücke **94**
**broccoli** der Brokkoli **48**
**broken arm** (der) gebrochene Arm **61**
**broom** der Besen **16**
**brother** der Bruder **8**
**brown** braun **117**
**bruise** (der) blaue Fleck **61**
**bucket** der Eimer **82**
**budgie** der Wellensittich **62**

**buggy** der Buggy **82**
**builder** der Bauarbeiter **102**
**building** das Gebäude **94**
**bus** der Bus **100**
**bus driver** der Busfahrer **102**
**bush** der Busch **90**
**butter** die Butter **50**
**button** der Knopf **35**
**(to) buy** kaufen **41, 46**
**(to) buy a ticket** eine Fahrkarte kaufen **97**

## C

**calculator** der Taschenrechner **27**
**calendar** der Kalender **106**
**calf** das Kalb **88**
**can** können **124**
**candle** die Kerze **113**
**cap** die Kappe **35**
**car** das Auto **100**
**caravan** das Wohnmobil **100**
**caretaker** der Hausmeister **24**
**carpet** der Teppich **12**
**carrot** die Karotte **49**
**(to) carry** tragen **46**
**cat** die Katze **62, 88**
**cauliflower** der Blumenkohl **48**
**CD player** der CD-Spieler **27**
**cellar** der Keller **10**
**chair** der Stuhl **17, 27**
**chalk** die Kreide **27**
**champion** der Champion **72**
**changing room** die Umkleidekabine **34**
**cheap** billig **34, 81**
**cheese** der Käse **50**
**cherry** die Kirsche **47**
**chest** die Brust **59**
**chest of drawers** die Kommode **13**
**chick** das Küken **88**
**chicken** das Hühnchen **50**
**child** das Kind **102**
**children** die Kinder **102**
**chimney** der Schornstein **10**
**chin** das Kinn **58**
**chips** die Pommes frites **50**
**chocolate** die Schokolade **50**
**Christmas carol** das Weihnachtslied **113**
**Christmas tree** der Weihnachtsbaum **113**
**church** die Kirche **98**
**cinema** das Kino **98**
**circle** der Kreis **121**
**city** die (Innen)Stadt **94**
**classroom** das Klassenzimmer **24**
**claw** die Kralle **64**
**clean** sauber **80**
**(to) clear out** ausmisten **87**
**(to) climb** klettern **77**
**climbing frame** das Klettergerüst **82**
**clock** die Uhr **27**
**closed** geschlossen **46**
**clothes hanger** der Kleiderbügel **34**
**cloud** die Wolke **90, 114**
**cloudy** wolkig **114**
**coach** der Trainer **72**
**coat** der Mantel **35**
**cock** der Hahn **88**
**coffee** der Kaffee **53**
**coke** die Cola **53**
**cold** kalt **114**
**(to) collect** sammeln **68, 87**
**(to) collect stickers** Aufkleber sammeln **68**
**(to) colour** anmalen **30**
**coloured pencil** der Buntstift **26**
**comb** der Kamm **14**
**compound** das Gehege **76**
**computer** der Computer **12, 27**
**computer game** das Computerspiel **28**
**cook** der Koch **103**
**cooker** der Herd **16**
**cornflakes** die Cornflakes **50**
**(to) cough** husten **57**
**cough** der Husten **61**
**cousin** der Kusin **9**
**cow** die Kuh **88**
**cream** die Sahne **50**
**crisps** die Chips **50**
**crocodile** das Krokodil **78**
**cross** das Kreuz **121**
**crowded** voll **46**
**crown** die Krone **112**
**cucumber** die Gurke **49**
**cup** die Tasse **16**

**cupboard** der Küchenschrank **16**
**curtain** der Vorhang **13**
**customer** der Kunde **34**
**cycle lane** der Fahrradweg **94**
**cyclist** der Radfahrer **94**
**cylinder** der Zylinder **121**

## D

**daffodil** die Osterglocke **110**
**(to) dance** tanzen **68**
**daughter** die Tochter **9**
**day** der Tag **108**
**December** Dezember **107**
**deer** der Hirsch **78**
**dentist** der Zahnarzt **56**
**desk** der Schreibtisch **12, 28**
**diamond** der Diamant **121**
**dice** die Würfel **28**
**dictionary** das Wörterbuch **28**
**dining room** das Esszimmer **10**
**dirty** schmutzig **80**
**dishwasher** die Geschirrspülmaschine **16**
**divided by** geteilt durch **120**
**(to) do** machen **19**
**(to) do ballet** Ballett machen **68**
**doctor** die Ärztin **56**
**dog** der Hund **62, 88**
**doll** die Puppe **82**
**dolphin** der Delfin **78**
**(to) do Maths** rechnen **30**
**donkey** der Esel **88**
**door** die Tür **11**
**doorbell** die Türklingel **11**
**(to) do the dishes** abwaschen **19**
**downstairs** unten **20**
**(to) draw** zeichnen **30**
**dress** das Kleid **35**
**(to) drink** trinken **65**
**driver** der Fahrer **94**
**dry** trocken **81, 114**
**(to) dry the dishes** abtrocknen **19**
**duck** die Ente **88**
**dunghill** der Misthaufen **86**

## E

**ear** das Ohr **58, 64**
**early** früh **109**
**earring** der Ohrring **39**
**Easter basket** der Osterkorb **110**
**Easter bunny** der Oster-hase **110**
**Easter egg** das Osterei **110**
**(to) eat** fressen **65**
**egg** das Ei **51**
**eight** acht **116**
**eighteen** achtzehn **118**
**eighty** achtzig **119**
**elbow** der Ellbogen **59**
**elephant** der Elefant **78**
**eleven** elf **118**
**empty** leer **46**
**English** Englisch **25**
**entrance** der Eingang **45**
**eraser** der Tafelschwamm **28**
**(to) examine** untersuchen **63**
**exercise book** das Heft **28**
**exit** der Ausgang **45**
**expensive** teuer **34, 81**
**(to) explain** erklären **30**
**eye** das Auge **58, 64**
**eye lashes** die Wimpern **58**

## F

**face** das Gesicht **58**
**factory** die Fabrik **98**
**family** die Familie **8**
**farmhouse** das Bauernhaus **86**
**fast** schnell **73, 80**
**father** der Vater **8**
**Father Christmas** der Weihnachtsmann **113**
**February** Februar **106**
**(to) feed** füttern **63, 87**
**feeding time** die Fütterung **76**
**feet** die Füße **60**
**felt-tip** der Filzstift **26**
**fence** der Zaun **21, 76**
**field** das Feld **90**
**fifteen** fünfzehn **118**
**fifty** fünfzig **119**
**finger** der Finger **60**
**fire engine** das Feuerwehrauto **100**
**firefighter** der Feuerwehrmann **103**
**fireplace** der Kamin **11**
**first** erster **73**
**fish** der Fisch **51, 62**
**five** fünf **116**

**flat** die Wohnung **20, 94**
**flour** das Mehl **51**
**flower** die Blume **21, 90**
**flowerbed** das Blumenbeet **21**
**(to) fly** fliegen **65**
**fog** der Nebel **114**
**foggy** neblig **114**
**folder** der Ordner **28**
**foot** der Fuß **60**
**football** Fußball **70**
**forest** der Wald **90**
**fork** die Gabel **17**
**forty** vierzig **119**
**fountain** der Brunnen **94**
**four** vier **116**
**fourteen** vierzehn **118**
**Friday** Freitag **108**
**fridge** der Kühlschrank **16**
**front door** die Haustür **11**
**frozen foods** die Tiefkühlkost **51**
**fruit** das Obst **47**
**fur** das Fell **64**
**furniture** die Möbel **12**

## G

**game** das Spiel **72**
**garage** die Garage **11**
**garden** der Garten **11**
**gate** das Tor **76**
**geese** die Gänse **89**
**gerbil** die Wüstenspringmaus **62**
**German** Deutsch **25**
**(to) get off** aussteigen **97**
**(to) get on** einsteigen **97**
**ghost** der Geist **111**
**giraffe** die Giraffe **78**
**girl** das Mädchen **24, 102**
**(to) give an injection** (eine) Spritze geben **63**
**glass** das Glas **17**
**globe** der Globus **28**
**gloves** die Handschuhe **36**
**glue** der Kleber **26**
**goat** die Ziege **88**
**(to) go by ...** (mit etwas) fahren **97**
**goldfish** der Goldfisch **62**
**golf** Golf **70**
**goose** die Gans **89**
**(to) go shopping** einkaufen gehen **46**
**(to) go sightseeing** Sehenswürdigkeiten ansehen **97**
**grandfather** der Großvater **8**
**grandmother** die Großmutter **8**
**grapes** die Weintrauben **47**
**grass** das Gras **90**
**green** grün **117**
**grey** grau **114**
**(to) guess** raten **30**
**guest** der Gast **112**
**guinea pig** das Meerschweinchen **62**
**gym** die Sporthalle **24**
**gymnastics** Gymnastik **70**

## H

**hair** die Haare **58**
**hairbrush** die Bürste **14**
**hairdresser** die Friseurin **103**
**hall** die Diele **10**
**Halloween** Halloween **111**
**ham** der Schinken **51**
**hamster** der Hamster **62**
**hand** die Hand **60**
**handbag** die Handtasche **38**
**happy** glücklich **73**
**(to) harvest** ernten **87**
**hat** der Hut **36**
**(to) have got** haben **44, 123**
**he** er **122**
**head** der Kopf **58**
**headache** die Kopfschmerzen **61**
**headmistress** die Schulleiterin **24**
**(to) hear** hören **57**
**heart** das Herz **121**
**helicopter** der Hubschrauber **100**
**(to) help** helfen **30, 57**
**hen** das Huhn **88**
**her** ihr **122**
**hill** der Hügel **90**
**him** ihm **122**
**hippo** das Nilpferd **78**
**his** sein **122**
**hockey** Hockey **70**
**honey** der Honig **51**
**hood** die Kapuze **36**
**hopscotch** das Hüpfspiel **82**
**horse** das Pferd **89**
**horseback riding** Reiten **70**
**hospital** das Krankenhaus **98**
**hot** heiß **114**

**hot chocolate** der Kakao **53**
**hotel** das Hotel **98**
**house** das Haus **20, 95**
**house number** die Hausnummer **20**
**How many?** Wie viele? **44, 125**
**How much?** Wie viel? **44, 125**
**husband** der Ehemann **9**

## I

**I** ich **122**
**ice cream** das Eis **51**
**ice hockey** Eishockey **70**
**(to) ice-skate** eislaufen **68**
**in** in **18**
**in front of** vor **18**
**inline skates** die Inliner **100**
**in the afternoon** am Nachmittag **109**
**in the evening** am Abend **109**
**in the morning** am Morgen **109**
**invitation** die Einladung **112**
**is** ist, ist gleich **8, 120**
**it** es, ihm **122**
**its** sein(e) **122**

## J

**jam** die Marmelade **51**
**January** Januar **106**
**(a pair of) jeans** die Jeans **36**
**judo** Judo **71**
**juice** der Saft **53**
**July** Juli **107**
**(to) jump** springen **65**
**junction** die Kreuzung **95**
**June** Juni **107**

## K

**kangaroo** das Känguruh **78**
**kennel** die Hundehütte **86**
**key** der Schlüssel **12**
**kitchen** die Küche **10**
**kite** der Drachen **82**
**knee** das Knie **60**
**knife** das Messer **17**
**knives** die Messer **17**

## L

**laces** die Schuhbänder **38**
**ladder** die Leiter **21**
**lake** der See **90**
**lamb** das Lamm **89**
**lamp** die Lampe **13**
**last** letzter **73**
**late** spät **109**
**lawn** der Rasen **21**
**(to) lay the table** (den) Tisch decken **19**
**leaf** das Blatt **90**
**(to) learn** lernen **30**
**leaves** die Blätter **90**
**left** links **96**
**leg** das Bein **60**
**lemon** die Zitrone **47**
**less** weniger **120**
**lesson** die Schulstunde **24**
**letterbox** der Briefkasten **11, 95**
**lettuce** der Salat **49**
**library** die Bücherei **98**
**lion** der Löwe **78**
**(to) listen to** zuhören **30**
**(to) live** leben **20, 97**
**living room** das Wohnzimmer **10**
**lizard** die Eidechse **78**
**long** lang **80**
**(to) look** aussehen **41**
**(to) look at** ansehen **77**
**(to) look for something** (etwas) suchen **19**
**lorry** der Lastwagen **100**
**loser** der Verlierer **72**
**loud** laut **81**

## M

**man** der Mann **102**
**map** die Landkarte **28**
**March** März **106**
**marmalade** die Orangenmarmelade **52**
**Maths** Mathe **25**
**May** Mai **107**
**me** mir **122**
**meadow** die Wiese **91**
**meat** das Fleisch **52**
**(to) meet friends** Freunde treffen **68**
**melon** die Melone **47**
**mice** die Mäuse **89**
**(to) milk** melken **87**
**milk** die Milch **52**
**minus** minus **120**
**mirror** der Spiegel **14**

**mittens** die Fäustlinge **36**
**Monday** Montag **108**
**money** das Geld **34**
**month** der Monat **106**
**more** mehr **120**
**mother** die Mutter **8**
**motorbike** das Motorrad **101**
**mouse** die Maus **62, 89**
**mouth** der Mund **58**; die Schnauze **64**
**multiplied with** mal **120**
**mummy** die Mumie **111**
**mushroom** der Pilz **49**
**Music** Musik **25**
**my** mein **122**


## N

**near** in der Nähe von **18**
**neck** der Hals **58**
**necklace** die Kette **39**
**neighbour** der Nachbar **20**
**nest** das Nest **110**
**new** neu **40, 80**
**next to** neben **18**
**nine** neun **116**
**nineteen** neunzehn **118**
**ninety** neunzig **119**
**no** nein **44, 122, 123, 124**
**noon** Mittag **109**
**nose** die Nase **58**
**(to) not feel well** (sich) nicht gut fühlen **57**
**November** November **107**
**nurse** die Krankenschwester **56**
**nut** die Nuss **51**


## O

**October** Oktober **107**
**office building** das Bürogebäude **98**
**old** alt **40, 80, 81**
**on** auf **18**
**one** eins **116**
**one hundred** hundert **119**
**one thousand** tausend **119**
**onion** die Zwiebel **49**
**on sale** im Angebot **34**
**on the left** auf der linken Seite **96**
**on the right** auf der rechten Seite **96**
**open** geöffnet **46**
**opposite** gegenüber **18**
**orange** die Apfelsine **47**; orange **117**
**our** unser **122**


## P

**packet** die Packung **45**
**(to) paint** malen **69**
**paintbox** der Malkasten **29**
**paintbrush** der Pinsel **28**
**pan** die Pfanne **16**
**panda** der Panda **79**
**parents** die Eltern **8**
**parrot** der Papagei **62, 79**
**path** der Weg **76**
**patient** der Patient **56**
**pavement** der Bürgersteig **95**
**paw** die Pfote **64**
**(to) pay** bezahlen **41**
**PE (Physical Education)** Sport **25**
**pea** die Erbse **49**
**peach** der Pfirsich **47**
**peacock** der Pfau **79**
**peanut butter** die Erdnussbutter **52**
**pear** die Birne **48**
**pedestrian** der Fußgänger **95**
**pedestrian zone** die Fußgängerzone **95**
**pen** der Füller **26**
**pencil** der Bleistift **26**
**pencil case** die Federmappe **26**
**penguin** der Pinguin **79**
**people** die Menschen **102**
**pepper** die Paprika **49**
**(to) pet** streicheln **63**
**pet** Haustier **123**
**petrol station** die Tankstelle **99**
**petting zoo** der Streichelzoo **76**
**pharmacist** die Apothekerin **56**
**pharmacy** die Apotheke **98**
**piano** das Klavier **29**
**(to) pick** pflücken **87**
**picnic rug** die Picknickdecke **82**
**(piece of) paper** das Papier **29**
**pig** das Schwein **89**
**piggy bank** das Sparschwein **13**
**piglet** das Ferkel **89**
**pigsty** der Schweinestall **86**
**pillow** das Kissen **13**

**pineapple** die Ananas **48**
**pizza** die Pizza **52**
**plaid** kariert **40**
**plain-coloured** einfarbig **40**
**plane** das Flugzeug **101**
**(to) plant** pflanzen **87**
**plaster** das Pflaster **61**
**plastic bag** die Plastiktüte **45**
**plate** der Teller **17**
**(to) play** spielen **19**
**(to) play chess** Schach spielen **68**
**player** der Spieler **72**
**(to) play football** Fußball spielen **68**
**playground** der Schulhof **24**
**playing field** das Spielfeld **72**
**(to) play the recorder** Flöte spielen **68**
**plum** die Pflaume **48**
**plus** plus **120**
**pocket** die Hosentasche **39**
**pointer** der Zeigestab **29**
**polar bear** der Eisbär **79**
**police car** das Polizeiauto **101**
**policeman** der Polizist **103**
**policewoman** die Polizistin **103**
**polka-dotted** gepunktet **40**
**pond** der Teich **91**
**pool** das Becken **76**
**poster** das Poster **29**
**postman** der Briefträger **103**
**post office** die Post **99**
**pot** der Topf **16**
**potato** die Kartoffel **49**
**prescription** das Rezept **56**
**present** das Geschenk **113**
**pretty** hübsch **40**
**price** der Preis **34**
**price tag** das Preisschild **34**
**puddle** die Pfütze **91**
**pullover** der Pullover **36**
**pumpkin** der Kürbis **111**
**pupil** der Schüler **24**
**purple** lila **117**
**purse** das Portemonnaie **39**
**(to) push** schieben **46**
**(to) put on** anziehen **41**
**pyjamas** der Schlafanzug **36**
**pyramid** die Pyramide **121**

## Q

**(to) queue** (sich) anstellen **97**
**quiet** leise **81**

## R

**rabbit** das Kaninchen **63**
**rabbit hutch** der Kaninchen-stall **86**
**race** das Rennen **72**
**radio** das Radio **12**
**rain** der Regen **91, 114**
**rainbow** der Regenbogen **91, 114**
**raincoat** der Regenmantel **36**
**rainy** regnerisch **115**
**raspberry** die Himbeere **48**
**(to) read** lesen **31, 68**
**rectangle** das Rechteck **121**
**red** rot **117**
**referee** der Schiedsrichter **72**
**reindeer** das Rentier **113**
**(to) repair** reparieren **87**
**restaurant** das Restaurant **99**
**ribbon** das Geschenkband **112**
**rice** der Reis **52**
**(to) ride a bike** Rad fahren **69, 97**
**(to) ride a horse** reiten **69, 87**
**right** rechts **96**
**ring** der Ring **39**
**river** der Fluss **91**
**roll** das Brötchen **52**
**roof** das Dach **11**
**room** das Zimmer **10**
**roundabout** das Karussell **82**
**rubber** der Radiergummi **26**
**rucksack** der Rucksack **38**
**rug** der Teppich **12**
**ruler** das Lineal **26**
**(to) run** rennen **65**
**running** Laufen **71**

## S

**sad** traurig **73, 81**
**sailing** Segeln **71**
**salami** die Salami **52**
**(a pair of) sandals** die Sandalen **38**

**sandbox** die Sandkiste **83**
**sand castle** die Sandburg **83**
**sandwich** das Sandwich **52**
**Saturday** Samstag **108**
**scarecrow** die Vogelscheuche **86**
**scarf** der Schal **36**
**school** die Schule **99**
**schoolbag** die Schultasche **29**
**(a pair of) scissors** die Schere **26**
**scooter** der Roller **101**
**(to) scratch** kratzen **65**
**seal** der Seehund **79**
**season** die Jahreszeit **106**
**secretary** die Sekretärin **56**
**see-saw** die Wippe **83**
**September** September **107**
**seven** sieben **116**
**seventeen** siebzehn **118**
**seventy** siebzig **119**
**shampoo** das Shampoo **15**
**sharpener** der Anspitzer **26**
**she** sie **122**
**shed** das Gartenhaus **21**
**sheep** das Schaf **89**
**shelf** das Regal **29**
**shelves** die Regale **29**
**ship** das Schiff **101**
**shirt** das Hemd **36**
**(a pair of) shoes** die Schuhe **38**
**shop** das Geschäft **99**
**shop assistant** Verkäufer(in) **34**
**shopping basket** der Einkaufskorb **45**
**short** kurz **80**
**shoulder** die Schulter **60**
**shower** die Dusche **15**
**showtime** die Vorführung **76**
**sign** das Schild **76**
**(to) sing** singen **31, 69**
**sink** die Spüle **16**
**sister** die Schwester **8**
**(to) sit down** (sich) hinsetzen **31**
**six** sechs **116**
**sixteen** sechzehn **118**
**sixty** sechzig **119**
**(to) skate** skaten **69**
**skiing** Skifahren **71**
**skipping rope** das Springseil **83**
**skirt** der Rock **37**
**sky** der Himmel **91**
**(to) sleep** schlafen **19**
**sleigh** der Schlitten **113**
**slide** die Rutsche **83**
**(a pair of) slippers** die Hausschuhe **38**
**slow** langsam **73, 80**
**small** klein **80**
**(to) smell** riechen **57**
**snake** die Schlange **79**
**(to) sneeze** niesen **57**
**snow** der Schnee **115**
**soap** die Seife **15**
**Social Studies and Sciences** Sachunterricht **25**
**(a pair of) socks** die Strümpfe **37**
**sofa** das Sofa **14**
**son** der Sohn **9**
**sore throat** die Halsschmer--zen **61**
**soup** die Suppe **52**
**spade** die Schaufel **83**
**spaghetti** die Spaghetti **53**
**(to) spell** buchstabieren **31**
**spider** die Spinne **63, 111**
**spoon** der Löffel **17**
**spring** der Frühling **106**
**square** das Quadrat **121**
**stable** der Stall **86**
**stadium** das Stadion **99**
**staircase** die Treppe **12**
**(to) stand up** aufstehen **31**
**stocking** der Strumpf **113**
**stomach ache** die Bauchschmerzen **61**
**storm** der Sturm **115**
**straight ahead** geradeaus **96**
**strawberry** die Erdbeere **48**
**street** die Straße **20**
**street light** die Straßenlaterne **95**
**street sign** das Straßenschild **95**
**striped** gestreift **40**
**sugar** der Zucker **53**
**suitcase** der Koffer **39**
**summer** der Sommer **106**
**sun** die Sonne **91, 115**
**Sunday** Sonntag **108**
**sunny** sonnig **115**

**supermarket** der Supermarkt **45, 99**
**surgery** die Arztpraxis **56**
**sweatshirt** das Sweatshirt **37**
**(to) swim** schwimmen **65**
**swimming** Schwimmen **71**
**swimming pool** das Schwimmbad **99**
**swing** die Schaukel **83**

## T

**table** der Tisch **17**
**table tennis** Tischtennis **71**
**tail** der Schwanz **64**
**(to) take care of** (sich) kümmern um **63**
**(to) take off** ausziehen **41**
**(to) talk** sprechen **31**
**tap** der Wasserhahn **15**
**(to) taste** schmecken **57**
**taxi** das Taxi **101**
**tea** der Tee **53**
**teacher** Lehrer(in) **24, 103**
**team** die Mannschaft **72**
**teaspoon** der Teelöffel **17**
**teddy bear** der Teddy **83**
**teeth** die Zähne **59**
**telephone** das Telefon **12**
**ten** zehn **116**
**tennis** Tennis **71**
**their** ihr **122**
**them** ihnen **122**
**they** sie **122**
**(to) think** denken **31**
**thirteen** dreizehn **118**
**thirty** dreißig **119**
**three** drei **116**
**(to) throw** werfen **77**
**thumb** der Daumen **60**
**Thursday** Donnerstag **108**
**ticket** die Eintrittskarte **76**
**ticket office** der Kartenschalter **77**
**ticket officer** der Kartenverkäufer **77**
**(to) tidy up** aufräumen **19**
**tie** die Krawatte **37**
**(to) tie the laces** Schuhbänder binden **41**
**tiger** der Tiger **79**
**(a pair of) tights** die Strumpfhose **37**
**timetable** der Stundenplan **25**
**today** heute **110**
**toe** der Zeh **60**
**toilet** die Toilette **15**
**toilet paper** das Toilettenpapier **15**
**tomato** die Tomate **49**
**tomorrow** morgen **110**
**too big** zu groß **40**
**too small** zu klein **40**
**tooth** der Zahn **59**
**toothache** die Zahnschmerzen **61**
**toothbrush** die Zahnbürste **15**
**toothpaste** die Zahnpasta **15**
**tortoise** die Schildkröte **63**
**(to) touch** berühren **57**
**town** die Stadt **96**
**toy car** das Spielzeugauto **83**
**toys** die Spielsachen **12**
**traffic light** die Ampel **96**
**traffic sign** das Verkehrsschild **95**
**train** der Zug **101**
**(a pair of) trainers** die Turnschuhe **38**
**train station** der Bahnhof **99**
**tram** die Straßenbahn **101**
**treat** die Süßigkeit **111**
**tree** der Baum **21, 91**
**tree house** das Baumhaus **21**
**triangle** das Dreieck **121**
**trick** der Streich **111**
**trolley** der Einkaufswagen **45**
**(a pair of) trousers** die Hose **37**
**(to) try on** anprobieren **41**
**Tuesday** Dienstag **108**
**tulip** die Tulpe **110**
**TV** der Fernseher **14**
**twelve** zwölf **118**
**twenty** zwanzig **118**
**two** zwei **116**

## U

**ugly** hässlich **40**
**uncle** der Onkel **9**
**under** unter **18**
**underground** die U-Bahn **101**
**underwear** die Unterwäsche **37**
**upstairs** oben **20**
**us** uns **122**

## V

**vacuum cleaner** der Staubsauger **16**
**vegetable patch** das Gemüsebeet **86**
**vet** der Tierarzt **56**
**village** das Dorf **96**
**(to) visit** besuchen **77**
**visitor** der Besucher **77**
**volleyball** Volleyball **71**

## W

**waiter** der Kellner **103**
**waiting room** das Wartezimmer **56**
**(to) wait in line** in der Schlange warten **46**
**waitress** die Kellnerin **103**
**(to) walk** gehen **97**
**wardrobe** der Kleiderschrank **13**
**warm** warm **115**
**washing machine** die Waschmaschine **15**
**(to) watch** bewachen **86**
**watch** die Armbanduhr **39**
**(to) watch TV** fernsehen **19**
**water** das Wasser **53**
**watermelon** die Wassermelone **48**
**we** wir **122**
**(to) wear** tragen **41**
**Wednesday** Mittwoch **108**
**week** die Woche **108**
**weekend** das Wochenende **108**
**wet** nass **81, 115**
**What?** Was? **125**
**When?** Wann? **125**
**Where?** Wo? **18, 44, 125**
**Which?** Welche? **125**
**whiskers** die Barthaare **64**
**(to) whisper** flüstern **31**
**white** weiß **117**
**Who?** Wer? **125**
**Why?** Warum? **125**
**wife** die Ehefrau **9**
**wind** der Wind **115**
**window** das Fenster **11**
**windsurfing** Windsurfen **71**
**windy** windig **115**
**wing** der Flügel **64**
**winner** der Sieger **72**
**winter** der Winter **106**
**witch** die Hexe **111**
**wolf** der Wolf **79**
**woman** die Frau **102**
**woolly hat** die Mütze **37**
**wrapping paper** das Geschenkpapier **112**
**(to) write** schreiben **31**

## Y

**yellow** gelb **117**
**yes** ja **44, 122, 123, 124**
**yesterday** gestern **110**
**you** du, dir, euch, ihr **122**
**young** jung **81**
**your** dein, euer **122**

## Z

**zebra crossing** der Zebrastreifen **96**
**(to) zip** den Reißverschluss zumachen **41**
**zipper** der Reißverschluss **37**
**zoo keeper** der Tierpfleger **77**

# Glossar Deutsch-Englisch

## A

**abwaschen** (to) do the dishes **19**
**abtrocknen** (to) dry the dishes **19**
**acht** eight **116**
**achtzehn** eighteen **118**
**achtzig** eighty **119**
**Adresse** address **20**
**alt** old **40, 80, 81**
**am Abend** in the evening **109**
**am Morgen** in the morning **109**
**am Nachmittag** in the afternoon **109**
**Ampel** traffic light **96**
**Ananas** pineapple **48**
**anmalen** (to) colour **30**
**Anorak** anorak **35**
**anprobieren** (to) try on **41**
**ansehen** (to) look at **77**
**Anspitzer** sharpener **26**
**(sich) anstellen** (to) queue **97**
**antworten** (to) answer **30**
**anziehen** (to) put on **41**
**Apfel** apple **47**
**Apfelsine** orange **47**
**Apotheke** pharmacy **98**
**Apothekerin** pharmacist **56**
**April** April **107**
**Arm** arm **59**
**Armband** bracelet **39**
**Armbanduhr** watch **39**
**Arztpraxis** surgery **56**
**Ärztin** doctor **56**
**auf** on **18**
**auf der linken Seite** on the left **96**
**auf der rechten Seite** on the right **96**
**Aufkleber sammeln** (to) collect stickers **68**
**aufräumen** (to) tidy up **19**
**aufstehen** (to) stand up **31**
**Auge** eye **58, 64**
**August** August **107**
**Ausgang** exit **45**
**ausmisten** (to) clear out **87**
**aussehen** (to) look **41**
**aussteigen** (to) get off **97**
**ausziehen** (to) take off **41**
**Auto** car **100**

## B

**Baby** baby **8**
**Bäcker** baker **102**
**Bäckerei** bakery **98**
**Badeanzug** bathing suit **35**
**Badewanne** bathtub **14**
**Badezimmer** bathroom **10**
**Badminton** badminton **70**
**Bahnhof** train station **99**
**Ball** ball **82**
**Ballett machen** (to) do ballet **68**
**Banane** banana **47**
**Bank** bank **98**; bench **82, 94**
**Bär** bear **78**
**Barthaare** whiskers **64**
**Baseball** baseball **70**
**Basketball** basketball **70**
**Bauarbeiter** builder **102**
**Bauch** belly **59**
**Bauchschmerzen** stomach ache **61**
**Bauernhaus** farmhouse **86**
**Baum** tree **91, 21**
**Baumhaus** tree house **21**
**Becken** pool **76**
**Bein** leg **60**
**beißen** (to) bite **65**
**bellen** (to) bark **65**
**berühren** (to) touch **57**
**Besen** broom **16**
**besser** better **73**
**besuchen** (to) visit **77**
**Besucher** visitor **77**
**Bett** bed **13**
**bewachen** (to) watch **86**
**bezahlen** (to) pay **41**
**Bikini** bikini **35**
**billig** cheap **34, 81**
**bin** am **9**
**Birne** pear **48**
**Blatt** leaf **90**
**Blätter** leaves **90**
**blau** blue **117**
**(der) blaue Fleck** bruise **61**
**Bleistift** pencil **26**
**Blume** flower **21, 90**
**Blumenbeet** flowerbed **21**
**Blumenkohl** cauliflower **48**
**Bluse** blouse **35**
**Blut** blood **60**
**bluten** (to) bleed **57**
**Bohnen** beans **48**
**braun** brown **117**
**Briefkasten** letterbox **11, 95**
**Briefträger** postman **103**

**Brokkoli** broccoli **48**
**Brot** bread **50**
**Brötchen** roll **52**
**Brücke** bridge **94**
**Bruder** brother **8**
**Brunnen** fountain **94**
**Brust** chest **59**
**Buch** book **27**
**Bücherei** library **98**
**Bücherregal** bookcase **14**
**buchstabieren** (to) spell **31**
**Buggy** buggy **82**
**Buntstift** coloured pencil **26**
**Bürgersteig** pavement **95**
**Bürogebäude** office building **98**
**Bürste** hairbrush **14**
**Bus** bus **100**
**Busch** bush **90**
**Busfahrer** bus driver **102**
**Butter** butter **50**

## C

**CD-Spieler** CD player **27**
**Champion** champion **72**
**Chips** crisps **50**
**Cola** coke **53**
**Computer** computer **12, 27**
**Computerspiel** computer game **28**
**Cornflakes** cornflakes **50**

## D

**Dach** roof **11**
**Dachboden** attic **10**
**Daumen** thumb **60**
**Decke** blanket **13**
**dein** your **122**
**Delfin** dolphin **78**
**denken** (to) think **31**
**Deutsch** German **25**
**Dezember** December **107**
**Diamant** diamond **121**
**Diele** hall **10**
**Dienstag** Tuesday **108**
**dir** you **122**
**Donnerstag** Thursday **108**
**Dorf** village **96**
**Drachen** kite **82**
**drei** three **116**
**Dreieck** triangle **121**
**dreißig** thirty **119**
**dreizehn** thirteen **118**
**du** you **122**
**Dusche** shower **15**

## E

**Ehefrau** wife **9**
**Ehemann** husband **9**
**Ei** egg **51**
**Eidechse** lizard **78**
**Eimer** bucket **82**
**einfarbig** plain-coloured **40**
**Eingang** entrance **45**
**einkaufen gehen** (to) go shopping **46**
**Einkaufskorb** shopping basket **45**
**Einkaufswagen** trolley **45**
**Einladung** invitation **112**
**eins** one **116**
**einsteigen** (to) get on **97**
**Eintrittskarte** ticket **76**
**Eis** ice cream **51**
**Eisbär** polar bear **79**
**Eishockey** ice hockey **70**
**eislaufen** (to) ice-skate **68**
**Elefant** elephant **78**
**elf** eleven **118**
**Ellbogen** elbow **59**
**Eltern** parents **8**
**Engel** angel **113**
**Englisch** English **25**
**Ente** duck **88**
**er** he **122**
**Erbse** pea **49**
**Erdbeere** strawberry **48**
**Erdnussbutter** peanut butter **52**
**erklären** (to) explain **30**
**ernten** (to) harvest **87**
**erster** first **73**
**es** it **122**
**Esel** donkey **88**
**Esszimmer** dining room **10**
**euch** you **122**
**euer** yours **122**

## F

**(mit etwas) fahren** (to) go by … **97**
**Fahrer** driver **94**
**(eine) Fahrkarte kaufen** (to) buy a ticket **97**
**Fahrrad** bike **100**
**Fahrradweg** cycle lane **94**
**Familie** family **8**
**Fabrik** factory **98**
**Fäustlinge** mittens **36**
**Februar** February **106**
**Federmappe** pencil case **26**

**Feld** field **90**
**Fell** fur **64**
**Fenster** window **11**
**Ferkel** piglet **89**
**fernsehen** (to) watch TV **19**
**Fernseher** TV **14**
**Feuerwehrauto** fire engine **100**
**Feuerwehrmann** firefighter **103**
**Filzstift** felt-tip **26**
**Finger** finger **60**
**Fisch** fish **51, 62**
**Flasche** bottle **45**
**Fledermaus** bat **111**
**Fleisch** meat **52**
**fliegen** (to) fly **65**
**Flöte spielen** (to) play the recorder **68**
**Flügel** wing **64**
**Flugzeug** plane **101**
**Fluss** river **91**
**flüstern** (to) whisper **31**
**fragen** (to) ask **30**
**Frau** woman **102**
**Freitag** Friday **108**
**fressen** (to) eat **65**
**Freunde treffen** (to) meet friends **68**
**Friseurin** hairdresser **103**
**früh** early **109**
**Frühling** spring **106**
**Füller** pen **26**
**fünf** five **116**
**fünfzehn** fifteen **118**
**fünfzig** fifty **119**
**Fuß** foot **60**
**Fußball** football **70**
**Fußball spielen** (to) play football **68**
**Füße** feet **60**
**Fußgänger** pedestrian **95**
**Fußgängerzone** pedestrian zone **95**
**füttern** (to) feed **63, 87**
**Fütterung** feeding time **76**

## G

**Gabel** fork **17**
**Gang** aisle **45**
**Gans** goose **89**
**Gänse** geese **89**
**Garage** garage **11**
**Garten** garden **11**
**Gartenhaus** shed **21**
**Gast** guest **112**
**Gebäude** building **94**
**(der) gebrochene Arm** broken arm **61**
**Geburtstag** birthday **112**
**Geburtstagskuchen** birthday cake **112**
**Geburtstagskarte** birthday card **112**
**Geburtstagsparty** birthday party **112**
**gegenüber** opposite **18**
**Gehege** compound **76**
**gehen** (to) walk **97**
**Geist** ghost **111**
**gelb** yellow **117**
**Geld** money **34**
**Gemüsebeet** vegetable patch **86**
**geöffnet** open **46**
**gepunktet** polka-dotted **40**
**geradeaus** straight ahead **96**
**Geschäft** shop **99**
**Geschenk** present **113**
**Geschenkband** ribbon **112**
**Geschenkpapier** wrapping paper **112**
**Geschirrspülmaschine** dishwasher **16**
**geschlossen** closed **46**
**Gesicht** face **58**
**gestern** yesterday **110**
**gestreift** striped **40**
**geteilt durch** divided by **120**
**Giraffe** giraffe **78**
**Glas** glass **17**
**Globus** globe **28**
**glücklich** happy **73**
**Goldfisch** goldfish **62**
**Golf** golf **70**
**Gras** grass **90**
**grau** grey **114**
**groß** big **80**
**Großmutter** grandmother **8**
**Großvater** grandfather **8**
**grün** green **117**
**Gurke** cucumber **49**
**Gürtel** belt **35**
**Gymnastik** gymnastics **70**

## H

**Haare** hair **58**
**haben** (to) have got **44, 123**
**Hahn** cock **88**
**Halloween** Halloween **111**

**Hals** neck **58**
**Halsschmerzen** sore throat **61**
**Hamster** hamster **62**
**Hand** hand **60**
**Handtasche** handbag **38**
**Handschuhe** gloves **36**
**hässlich** ugly **40**
**Haus** house **20, 95**
**Hausmeister** caretaker **24**
**Hausnummer** house number **20**
**Hausschuhe** (a pair of) slippers **38**
**Haustier** pet **123**
**Haustür** front door **11**
**Heft** exercise book **28**
**heiß** hot **114**
**helfen** (to) help **30, 57**
**Hemd** shirt **36**
**Herbst** autumn **106**
**Herd** cooker **16**
**Herz** heart **121**
**heute** today **110**
**Hexe** witch **111**
**Himbeere** raspberry **48**
**Himmel** sky **91**
**(sich) hinsetzen** (to) sit down **31**
**hinter** behind **18**
**Hirsch** deer **78**
**Hockey** hockey **70**
**Honig** honey **51**
**hören** (to) hear **57**
**Hose** (a pair of) trousers **37**
**Hosentasche** pocket **39**
**Hotel** hotel **98**
**hübsch** pretty **40**
**Hubschrauber** helicopter **100**
**Hügel** hill **90**
**Huhn** hen **88**
**Hühnchen** chicken **50**
**Hund** dog **62, 88**
**Hundehütte** kennel **86**
**hundert** one hundred **119**
**Hüpfspiel** hopscotch **82**
**husten** (to) cough **57**
**Husten** cough **61**
**Hut** hat **36**

## I

**ich** I **122**
**ihm** him, it **122**
**ihnen** them **122**
**ihr** her, you, their **122**
**im Angebot** on sale **34**
**in** in **18**
**in der Nacht** at night **109**
**in der Nähe von** near **18**
**in der Schlange warten** (to) wait in line **46**
**Inliner** inline skates **100**
**(Innen)Stadt** city **94**
**ist** is **8**
**ist gleich** is **120**

## J

**ja** yes **44, 122, 123, 124**
**Jahreszeit** season **106**
**Januar** January **106**
**Jeans** (a pair of) jeans **36**
**Judo** judo **71**
**Juli** July **107**
**jung** young **81**
**Junge** boy **24, 102**
**Juni** June **107**

## K

**Kaffee** coffee **53**
**Kakao** hot chocolate **53**
**Kalb** calf **88**
**Kalender** calendar **106**
**kalt** cold **114**
**Kamin** fireplace **11**
**Kamm** comb **14**
**Känguruh** kangaroo **78**
**Kaninchen** rabbit **63**
**Kaninchenstall** rabbit hutch **86**
**Kappe** cap **35**
**Kapuze** hood **36**
**kariert** plaid **40**
**Karotte** carrot **49**
**Kartenschalter** ticket office **77**
**Kartenverkäufer** ticket officer **77**
**Kartoffel** potato **49**
**Karussell** roundabout **82**
**Käse** cheese **50**
**Katze** cat **62, 88**
**kaufen** (to) buy **41, 46**
**Keks** biscuit **50**
**Keller** cellar **10**
**Kellner** waiter **103**
**Kellnerin** waitress **103**
**Kerze** candle **113**
**Kette** necklace **39**
**Kind** child **102**
**Kinder** children **102**
**Kinn** chin **58**
**Kino** cinema **98**

**Kirche** church **98**
**Kirsche** cherry **47**
**Kissen** pillow **13**
**Klassenzimmer** classroom **24**
**Klavier** piano **29**
**Kleber** glue **26**
**Kleid** dress **35**
**Kleiderbügel** clothes hanger **34**
**Kleiderschrank** wardrobe **13**
**klein** small **80**
**Klettergerüst** climbing frame **82**
**klettern** (to) climb **77**
**Knie** knee **60**
**Knopf** button **35**
**Koch** cook **103**
**Koffer** suitcase **39**
**Kommode** chest of drawers **13**
**können** can **124**
**Kopf** head **58**
**Kopfschmerzen** headache **61**
**Kralle** claw **64**
**Krankenhaus** hospital **98**
**Krankenschwester** nurse **56**
**Krankenwagen** ambulance **100**
**kratzen** (to) scratch **65**
**Krawatte** tie **37**
**Kreide** chalk **27**
**Kreis** circle **121**
**Kreuz** cross **121**
**Kreuzung** junction **95**
**Krokodil** crocodile **78**
**Krone** crown **112**
**Küche** kitchen **10**
**Küchenschrank** cupboard **16**
**Kuh** cow **88**
**Kühlschrank** fridge **16**
**Küken** chick **88**
**(sich) kümmern um** (to) take care of **63**
**Kunde** customer **34**
**Kunst** Art **25**
**Kürbis** pumpkin **111**
**kurz** short **80**
**Kusin** cousin **9**

## L

**Lamm** lamb **89**
**Lampe** lamp **13**
**Landkarte** map **28**
**lang** long **80**
**langsam** slow **73, 80**
**Lastwagen** lorry **100**
**Laufen** running **71**
**laut** loud **81**
**leben** (to) live **20, 97**
**leer** empty **46**
**Lehrer(in)** teacher **24, 103**
**Leichtathletik** athletics **70**
**leise** quiet **81**
**Leiter** ladder **21**
**lernen** (to) learn **30**
**lesen** (to) read **31, 68**
**letzter** last **73**
**lila** purple **117**
**Lineal** ruler **26**
**links** left **96**
**Löffel** spoon **17**
**Löwe** lion **78**
**Luftballon** balloon **112**

## M

**machen** (to) do **19**
**Mädchen** girl **24, 102**
**Mai** May **107**
**mal** multiplied with **120**
**malen** (to) paint **69**
**Malkasten** paintbox **29**
**Mann** man **102**
**Mannschaft** team **72**
**Mantel** coat **35**
**Marmelade** jam **51**
**März** March **106**
**Mathe** Maths **25**
**Maus** mouse **62, 89**
**Mäuse** mice **89**
**Meerschweinchen** guinea pig **62**
**Mehl** flour **51**
**mehr** more **120**
**Mehrfamilienhaus** block of flats **94**
**mein** my **122**
**melken** (to) milk **87**
**Melone** melon **47**
**Menschen** people **102**
**Messer** knife **17**
**Messer** knives **17**
**Milch** milk **52**
**minus** minus **120**
**mir** me **122**
**Misthaufen** dunghill **86**
**Mittag** noon **109**
**Mittwoch** Wednesday **108**
**Möbel** furniture **12**

**Monat** month **106**
**Montag** Monday **108**
**morgen** tomorrow **110**
**Motorrad** motorbike **101**
**Mumie** mummy **111**
**Mund** mouth **58**
**Musik** Music **25**
**Mutter** mother **8**
**Mütze** woolly hat **37**

## N

**Nachbar** neighbour **20**
**Nase** nose **58**
**nass** wet **81, 115**
**Nebel** fog **114**
**neben** next to **18**
**neblig** foggy **114**
**nein** no **44, 122, 123, 124**
**Nest** nest **110**
**neu** new **40, 80**
**neun** nine **116**
**neunzehn** nineteen **118**
**neunzig** ninety **119**
**(sich) nicht gut fühlen** (to) not feel well **57**
**niesen** (to) sneeze **57**
**Nilpferd** hippo **78**
**November** November **107**
**Nuss** nut **51**

## O

**Obst** fruit **47**
**oben** upstairs **20**
**Ohr** ear **58, 64**
**Ohrring** earring **39**
**Oktober** October **107**
**Onkel** uncle **9**
**orange** orange **117**
**Orangenmarmelade** marmalade **52**
**Ordner** folder **28**
**Osterei** Easter egg **110**
**Osterglocke** daffodil **110**
**Osterhase** Easter bunny **110**
**Osterkorb** Easter basket **110**

## P

**Packung** packet **45**
**Panda** panda **79**
**Papagei** parrot **62, 79**
**Papier** (piece of) paper **29**
**Papierkorb** bin **27**
**Paprika** pepper **49**
**Patient** patient **56**
**Pause** breaktime **25**
**Pfanne** pan **16**
**Pfau** peacock **79**
**Pferd** horse **89**
**Pfirsich** peach **47**
**pflanzen** (to) plant **87**
**Pflaster** plaster **61**
**Pflaume** plum **48**
**pflücken** (to) pick **87**
**Pfote** paw **64**
**Pfütze** puddle **91**
**Picknickdecke** picnic rug **82**
**Pilz** mushroom **49**
**Pinguin** penguin **79**
**Pinsel** paintbrush **28**
**Pizza** pizza **52**
**Plastiktüte** plastic bag **45**
**plus** plus **120**
**Po** bottom **59**
**Polizeiauto** police car **101**
**Polizist** policeman **103**
**Polizistin** policewoman **103**
**Pommes frites** chips **50**
**Portemonnaie** purse **39**
**Post** post office **99**
**Poster** poster **29**
**Preis** price **34**
**Preisschild** price tag **34**
**Pullover** pullover **36**
**Puppe** doll **82**
**Pyramide** pyramid **121**

## Q

**Quadrat** square **121**

## R

**Rad fahren** (to) ride a bike **69, 97**
**Radfahrer** cyclist **94**
**Radiergummi** rubber **26**
**Radio** radio **12**
**Rasen** lawn **21**
**raten** (to) guess **30**
**rechnen** (to) do Maths **30**
**Rechteck** rectangle **121**
**rechts** right **96**
**Regal** shelf **29**
**Regale** shelves **29**
**Regen** rain **91, 114**
**Regenbogen** rainbow **91, 114**
**Regenmantel** raincoat **36**
**regnerisch** rainy **115**
**Reis** rice **52**
**Reißverschluss** zipper **37**
**Reißverschluss zu machen** (to) zip **41**
**Reiten** horseback riding **70**

**reiten** (to) ride a horse **69, 87**
**Rennen** race **72**
**rennen** (to) run **65**
**Rentier** reindeer **113**
**reparieren** (to) repair **87**
**Restaurant** restaurant **99**
**Rezept** prescription **56**
**riechen** (to) smell **57**
**Ring** ring **39**
**Rock** skirt **37**
**Roller** scooter **101**
**rot** red **117**
**Rücken** back **59**
**Rucksack** rucksack **38**
**Ruderboot** boat **100**
**Rutsche** slide **83**

## S

**Sachunterricht** Social Studies and Sciences **25**
**Saft** juice **53**
**Sahne** cream **50**
**Salami** salami **52**
**Salat** lettuce **49**
**sammeln** (to) collect **68, 87**
**Samstag** Saturday **108**
**Sandalen** (a pair of) sandals **38**
**Sandburg** sand castle **83**
**Sandkiste** sandbox **83**
**Sandwich** sandwich **52**
**sauber** clean **80**
**Schach spielen** (to) play chess **68**
**Schaf** sheep **89**
**Schal** scarf **36**
**Schaufel** spade **83**
**Schaukel** swing **83**
**Schere** (a pair of) scissors **26**
**Scheune** barn **86**
**schieben** (to) push **46**
**Schiedsrichter** referee **72**
**Schiff** ship **101**
**Schild** sign **76**
**Schildkröte** tortoise **63**
**Schinken** ham **51**
**Schlafanzug** pyjamas **36**
**schlafen** (to) sleep **19**
**Schlafzimmer** bedroom **10**
**Schlange** snake **79**
**Schlitten** sleigh **113**
**Schlüssel** key **12**
**schmecken** (to) taste **57**
**schmutzig** dirty **80**
**Schnabel** beak **64**
**Schnauze** mouth **64**
**Schnee** snow **115**
**schnell** fast **73, 80**
**Schokolade** chocolate **50**
**Schornstein** chimney **10**
**schreiben** (to) write **31**
**Schreibtisch** desk **12, 28**
**Schuhbänder** laces **38**
**Schuhbänder binden** (to) tie the laces **41**
**Schuhe** (a pair of) shoes **38**
**Schule** school **99**
**Schüler** pupil **24**
**Schulhof** playground **24**
**Schulleiterin** headmistress **24**
**Schulstunde** lesson **24**
**Schultasche** schoolbag **29**
**Schulter** shoulder **60**
**Schwanz** tail **64**
**schwarz** black **117**
**Schwein** pig **89**
**Schweinestall** pigsty **86**
**Schwester** sister **8**
**Schwimmbad** swimming pool **99**
**Schwimmen** swimming **71**
**schwimmen** (to) swim **65**
**sechs** six **116**
**sechzehn** sixteen **118**
**sechzig** sixty **119**
**See** lake **90**
**Seehund** seal **79**
**Segeln** sailing **71**
**Sehenswürdigkeiten ansehen** (to) go sightseeing **97**
**Seife** soap **15**
**sein(e)** his, its **122**
**Sekretärin** secretary **56**
**September** September **107**
**Sessel** armchair **14**
**Shampoo** shampoo **15**
**sie** she, they **122**
**sieben** seven **116**
**siebzehn** seventeen **118**
**siebzig** seventy **119**
**Sieger** winner **72**
**sind** are **9**
**singen** (to) sing **31, 69**
**skaten** (to) skate **69**
**Skifahren** skiing **71**
**Sofa** sofa **14**
**so gut wie** as good as **73**
**Sohn** son **9**
**Sommer** summer **106**
**Sonne** sun **91, 115**

**sonnig** sunny **115**
**Sonntag** Sunday **108**
**Spaghetti** spaghetti **53**
**Sparschwein** piggy bank **13**
**spät** late **109**
**Spiegel** mirror **14**
**Spiel** game **72**
**spielen** (to) play **19**
**Spieler** player **72**
**Spielfeld** playing field **72**
**Spielsachen** toys **12**
**Spielzeugauto** toy car **83**
**Spinne** spider **63, 111**
**Sport** PE (Physical Education) **25**
**Sporthalle** gym **24**
**sprechen** (to) talk **31**
**springen** (to) jump **65**
**Springseil** skipping rope **83**
**(eine) Spritze geben** (to) give an injection **63**
**Spüle** sink **16**
**Stadion** stadium **99**
**Stadt** town **96**
**Stall** stable **86**
**Staubsauger** vacuum cleaner **16**
**Stiefel** (a pair of) boots **38**
**Straße** street **20**
**Straßenbahn** tram **101**
**Straßenlaterne** street light **95**
**Straßenschild** streetsign **95**
**Streich** trick **111**
**streicheln** (to) pet **63**
**Streichelzoo** petting zoo **76**
**Strumpf** stocking **113**
**Strümpfe** (a pair of) socks **37**
**Strumpfhose** (a pair of) tights **37**
**Stuhl** chair **17, 27**
**Stundenplan** timetable **25**
**Sturm** storm **115**
**(etwas) suchen** (to) look for something **19**
**Supermarkt** supermarket **45, 99**
**Suppe** soup **52**
**Süßigkeit** treat **111**
**Sweatshirt** sweatshirt **37**

## T

**Tafel** blackboard **27**; board **29**
**Tafelschwamm** eraser **28**
**Tag** day **108**
**Tankstelle** petrol station **99**
**Tante** aunt **9**
**tanzen** (to) dance **68**
**Tasche** bag **38**
**Taschenrechner** calculator **27**
**Tasse** cup **16**
**tausend** one thousand **119**
**Taxi** taxi **101**
**Teddy** teddy bear **83**
**Tee** tea **53**
**Teelöffel** teaspoon **17**
**Teich** pond **91**
**Telefon** telephone **12**
**Teller** plate **17**
**Teppich** carpet **12**; rug **12**
**teuer** expensive **34, 81**
**Tiefkühlkost** frozen foods **51**
**Tierarzt** vet **56**
**Tierpfleger** zoo keeper **77**
**Tiger** tiger **79**
**Tisch** table **17**
**(den) Tisch decken** (to) lay the table **19**
**Tischtennis** table tennis **71**
**Tochter** daughter **9**
**Toilette** toilet **15**
**Toilettenpapier** toilet paper **15**
**Tomate** tomato **49**
**Topf** pot **16**
**Tor** gate **76**
**tragen** (to) carry **46**; (to) wear **41**
**Trainer** coach **72**
**traurig** sad **73, 81**
**Treppe** staircase **12**
**trinken** (to) drink **65**
**trocken** dry **81, 114**
**Tulpe** tulip **110**
**Tür** door **11**
**Türklingel** doorbell **11**
**Turnschuhe** (a pair of) trainers **38**

## U

**U-Bahn** underground **101**
**Uhr** clock **27**
**um Mitternacht** at midnight **109**
**um … Uhr** at … o'clock **109**
**Umkleidekabine** changing room **34**
**uns** us **122**
**unser** our **122**

**unten** downstairs **20**
**unter** under **18**
**untersuchen** (to) examine **63**
**Unterwäsche** underwear **37**

## V

**Vater** father **8**
**Verband** bandage **61**
**Verkäufer(in)** shop assistant **34**
**Verkehrsschild** traffic sign **95**
**Verlierer** loser **72**
**vier** four **116**
**vierzehn** fourteen **118**
**vierzig** forty **119**
**Vogelhaus** bird house **21**
**Vogelscheuche** scarecrow **86**
**voll** crowded **46**
**Volleyball** volleyball **71**
**vor** in front of **18**
**Vorführung** showtime **76**
**Vorhang** curtain **13**

## W

**Wald** forest **90**
**Wann?** When? **125**
**warm** warm **115**
**Wartezimmer** waiting room **56**
**Warum?** Why? **125**
**Was?** What? **125**
**Waschbecken** basin **14**
**Waschmaschine** washing machine **15**
**Wasser** water **53**
**Wasserhahn** tap **15**
**Wassermelone** watermelon **48**
**Wecker** alarm clock **13**
**Weg** path **76**
**Weihnachtsbaum** Christmas tree **113**
**Weihnachtslied** Christmas carol **113**
**Weihnachtsmann** Father Christmas **113**
**Weintrauben** grapes **47**
**weiß** white **117**
**Welche?** Which? **125**
**Wellensittich** budgie **62**
**weniger** less **120**
**Wer?** Who? **125**
**werfen** (to) throw **77**
**Wiese** meadow **91**
**Wie viel?** How much? **44, 125**
**Wie viele?** How many? **44, 125**
**Wimpern** eye lashes **58**
**Wind** wind **115**
**windig** windy **115**
**Windsurfen** windsurfing **71**
**Winter** winter **106**
**Wippe** see-saw **83**
**wir** we **122**
**Wo?** Where? **18, 44, 125**
**Woche** week **108**
**Wochenende** weekend **108**
**Wohnmobil** caravan **100**
**Wohnung** flat **20, 94**
**Wohnzimmer** living room **10**
**Wolf** wolf **79**
**Wolke** cloud **90, 114**
**wolkig** cloudy **114**
**Wörterbuch** dictionary **28**
**Würfel** dice **28**
**Wüstenspringmaus** gerbil **62**
**wütend** angry **73**

## Z

**Zahn** tooth **59**
**Zahnarzt** dentist **56**
**Zahnbürste** toothbrush **15**
**Zähne** teeth **59**
**Zahnpasta** toothpaste **15**
**Zahnschmerzen** toothache **61**
**Zaun** fence **21, 76**
**Zebrastreifen** zebra crossing **96**
**Zeh** toe **60**
**Zehn** ten **116**
**zeichnen** (to) draw **30**
**Zeigestab** pointer **29**
**Ziege** goat **88**
**Zimmer** room **10**
**Zitrone** lemon **47**
**Zucker** sugar **53**
**Zug** train **101**
**zu groß** too big **40**
**zu Hause** at home **20**
**zuhören** (to) listen to **30**
**zu klein** too small **40**
**zwanzig** twenty **118**
**zwei** two **118**
**Zwiebel** onion **49**
**zwischen** between **18**
**zwölf** twelve **118**
**Zylinder** cylinder **121**